DISCARD

TRAINWRECK

TRAINWRECK

The Women We Love to Hate, Mock, and Fear...and Why

SADY DOYLE

MELVILLE HOUSE
BROOKLYN • LONDON

TRAINWRECK

First Melville House Printing: September 2016

Melville House Publishing   8 Blackstock Mews
          46 John Street   and   Islington
     Brooklyn, NY 11201   London N4 2BT

mhpbooks.com   facebook.com/mhpbooks   @melvillehouse

Library of Congress Cataloging-in-Publication Data
Names: Doyle, Sady, author.
Title: Trainwreck : the women we love to hate, mock, and
     fear . . . and why / Sady Doyle.
Description: Brooklyn : Melville House, [2016] | Includes
     bibliographical references and index.
Identifiers: LCCN 2016015117 (print) | LCCN 2016025264
     (ebook) | ISBN 9781612195636 (hardcover) | ISBN
     9781612195643 (ebook)
Subjects: LCSH: Women in mass media. | Celebrities—
     Conduct of life—Press coverage. | Celebrities—
     Conduct of life—Public opinion. | Women—Conduct
     of life—Press coverage. | Women—Conduct of life—
     Public opinion. |Feminist theory.
Classification: LCC P94.5.W65 D69 2016 (print) | LCC
     P94.5.W65 (ebook) | DDC 305.40973—dc23
LC record available at https://lccn.loc.gov/2016015117

Design by Marina Drukman

Printed in the United States of America

1 3 5 7 9 10 8 6 4 2

DISCARD

And if I am to speak of womanly virtues to those of you who will henceforth be widows, let me sum them up in one short admonition: To a woman not to show more weakness than is natural to her sex is a great glory, and not to be talked about for good or for evil among men.

—PERICLES, Funeral Oration

Q: What's the difference between Amy Winehouse and Amy Winehouse jokes?
A: The jokes will get old.

—Jokes4Us.com

CONTENTS

OUR TRAINWRECKS, OURSELVES

She's everywhere once you start looking for her: the trainwreck.

An actress known for light, bubbly romantic comedies and teen dramas throws a bong out of a thirty-sixth-floor window, to the dismay of assembled police officers. Her neighbors tell the press that she's been talking to herself, and that they suspect a psychotic break. A timeline of her "meltdown" appears on *Jezebel*. Late-night comedians have grist for months.

A reality-TV star appears on the cover of *Vogue*, causing massive backlash and speculation as to whether the magazine has "killed" its prestigious brand. The woman is rumored to have leaked her own sex tape. She once accepted thousands of dollars to accompany a wealthy man on a date. In the *Vogue* issue in question, she's posing with her fiancé and newborn child. Readers threaten to boycott the publication.

An actress's "fuck list," naming every man she's slept with, is circulated in advance of her upcoming reality series.

A musician's "fuck list," naming every man she's thought to have dated, is printed up in Helvetica font and sold as a T-shirt online.

A pop star known for her drug use and troubled relationship is found dead in her apartment.

A pop star known for her drug use and troubled relationship is found dead in her hotel bathtub.

A pop star known for her drug use and troubled relationship remains under her father's conservatorship due to mental incompetency. Ticket sales for her Las Vegas shows are through the roof.

It's easy to look at these women and see what they did wrong, tally up their sins and errors: insensitive, provocative, promiscuous, off-the-wagon, crazy. It's easy to tell yourself, *this is not my story.* But I'd wager good, hard money that, if you got the chance to speak to any of these women, they'd tell you that these are not their stories, either.

The privilege of controlling your own narrative is easy to take for granted. It's easy to confuse for a right; to assume that, of all the people in this loud and crowded world, you're the person best suited to tell the world who you are, or what you are, or what your actions and emotions mean in context.

Yet we know that narratives can be stolen, and weaponized. We've seen it happen again and again. Say the words "celebrity trainwreck," and the image immediately appears: young, pretty, most likely blond, and in some degree of high-gloss disarray, pinned between the club and the door of her limousine by a wall of flashing cameras. She's drunk, or she's high, or she's naked, or she's crying—or she will be, anyway, by the end of the night. The cameras are there to testify to her impending doom. They're there so we can watch it happen. Hence the etymology, actually—just as people are supposedly unable to avoid staring at a gruesome wreck on the highway, you know that this person is going to suffer, horribly, exceptionally, and you won't look away, because you enjoy it. The theft of narrative is where this begins, because, on some level, becoming a trainwreck simply means that the public assumes the right to control how you can define yourself: Kim Kardashian, for example, cannot be both the star of a sex tape and a blushing bride on the cover of *Vogue*. We'll mock and scorn her for being the one, but flat-out punish her and *Vogue* both if she attempts to be the other. It also means losing authority over your own decisions. Some lose that authority literally, by being put in jail or in hospitals or under the conservatorship of their parents, but more often, it's simply a matter of establishing them as "troubled"; as "out of control"; as people who don't know how to live their own lives.

But it escalates from there. All too often, losing your story also means that if you make decisions people don't like—after a certain point, in this process, every decision you make will be one people don't like—they feel entitled to hurt you. It means being subject to a hostile, unasked-for, all-consuming intimacy: having other people claim ownership over your body, your sexual history, your medical history, your emotional life, your future. Having them feel entitled to scream slurs at you, or threaten your life, or call your employer until you're unemployed, if you don't follow instructions. Nothing is off-limits: After Whitney Houston died, *ABC News* published the information that the coroner had found scars on her chest consistent with breast implants. It had nothing to do with her death—she had drowned, and breast implants have never, to my knowledge, risen up of their own accord and drowned their owner—but the world was, apparently, entitled to that information.

This isn't "the cost of fame," some necessary price one pays for being a public figure—or, if it is, it's only in the sense that everyone is a public figure, because it happens to "civilians," too—people who post unflattering pictures of themselves, or irritate one too many people with their personal blogs, or say stupid things on Twitter. And it isn't simply a matter of getting punished for wrongdoing—or, if it is, we should all be worried, because this specific wrongdoing tends to sneak up on people from behind, when they haven't intentionally or knowingly broken any rules. No one becomes a musician hoping to be placed on someone's celebrity death watch list. No one takes her first drink hoping to become an alcoholic. And no one—I am almost entirely certain—has ever had sex assuming that the experience will later be summarized on a popular novelty T-shirt.

And yet, here we are. With the stories we have; with the experience of constantly witnessing somebody else's wreckage. Once we start to realize that it can happen to anyone, we can begin to ask why it happens at all.

Envy is a powerful force. Traditionally, the trainwreck starts out as the girl who "has everything going for her": She is famous, after all, because she's attained some extremely rare level of professional success, and probably some of the wealth and adulation that goes along with it. Her implosion is a way of taking her back down a few notches, to where we live. The girl who "has everything" can have everything taken away.

This isn't entirely unfair. As long as we live in an unjust society, where the vast majority of us are struggling, and where ridiculously huge rewards are handed out for ridiculously stupid reasons—where pretending to be a sexy doctor on TV comes with more money, more praise, and vastly more publicity than actually going to med school and saving lives—it will always make some kind of sense to resent celebrities. The moralistic, concern-trolling quality of trainwreck coverage, the "What's Going to Come of Poor Dear Lindsay" factor, might just come down to our wanting to believe they "deserve" their fame. (As if anyone could possibly deserve such a thing; Leonardo DiCaprio has a private island, for God's sake. He wouldn't "deserve" that standard of living if he followed up each and every movie project by saving a busload of kindergarteners from going over a cliff.) We may just want to believe that the people we reward the most are the most deserving of being rewarded; that they got better lives by being better people. Which, in turn, makes our delight in celebrity suffering a form of vigilante justice: We're meting out what we believe to be just punishment of people enjoying a lifestyle that they haven't "earned," punishing flawed people to reaffirm our belief that celebrities must be better than human.

Or perhaps it comes down to a simple need to feel good about ourselves—a need to believe that someone else in this world is doing worse, or just *is* worse, than we are. It's an ugly little facet of human nature, but it's unavoidable: We define ourselves by exclusion, by rejecting or shaming others as a means of proving that we don't share their flaws. You might do it to drug users, or the mentally ill, or Republicans, but I've yet to meet anyone who doesn't do it. By zeroing in on the messiest and most badly behaved women, and rejecting them, we make a statement about what makes a woman good.

Or it could all come down to the "just world hypothesis": The social-psychology theory that if we see something bad happen to another human being, we assume that the person deserved it and start coming up with reasons. On some level, human beings are incapable of accepting that bad things happen for no reason. We have to assume that misfortune proceeds from personal flaw. Any other explanation is just too frightening: Whether you're getting threatened on Facebook, getting mugged on a street corner, or just getting a piano dropped on you from a great height, we assume you just shouldn't have posted that picture, lived in that neighborhood, or walked down that street on piano-moving day. If we believed anything else, we'd have to acknowledge that the universe is indifferent; that no benevolent force protects us from being mugged, threatened, or squashed. We'd have to acknowledge that we don't live in a just world.

So, we may wreck people simply to validate ourselves. We may wreck them because we're jealous. We may wreck them because we fear the sight of public suffering, or because, well, everyone else hates them, so they must have done something to deserve it. Maybe. But then, there's my favorite theory: Maybe we wreck people because they're women.

It's not that men can't be wrecked. There are plenty of male celebrities who have become the targets of full-scale, cross-culture hatred. But they usually have to work a lot harder for it: Chris Brown had to beat his girlfriend within an inch of her life. Justin Bieber and Michael Richards had to get caught dropping n-bombs. Mel Gibson had to terrorize his girlfriend, and also utter every ethnic and sexist slur in the books, on more than one occasion, over a period of years, before we gave him up. Conversely, just try asking people why they "hate" Katherine Heigl, or Kristen Stewart, or Anne Hathaway: She just seems arrogant. She just seems unpleasant. She just seems like she's trying too hard to be liked.

Men also have more options, in terms of redeeming themselves. It's easy to say that acts of open violence are the line to draw, but if you can even remember that the rugged-yet-sensitive heartthrob Josh Brolin was arrested on a domestic battery charge in 2004, you're a rare bird indeed. Bringing up the fact that Norman Mailer stabbed his wife will get you labeled a philistine, in some circles. Steven Tyler once adopted a sixteen-year-old girl in order to have sex with her, and for his crimes, we rewarded him with a judge slot on American Idol.

And, while I could try to find examples of famous men who have redeemed their reputations from wild behavior, promiscuous sex, and irresponsible drug use, research reveals that the answer is, roughly, all of them. In fact "redemption" seems like the wrong word for what happens to some of these guys: Keith Richards's drug career has included accidentally snorting strychnine, setting himself on fire on multiple occasions because he was so wasted he passed out while smoking a cigarette, and taking to the media in 2013 to defend heroin as essentially useful to the creative process. Hunter S. Thompson was best known for getting wasted on the job and living in a "fortified compound" stocked with dynamite and heavy firearms. Henry Miller wrote a modernist epic about how much fun it was to have sex with prostitutes. Members of Led Zeppelin once encouraged a woman to put a dead fish up her vagina. For all this, these guys became heroes: hard-living, boundary-pushing rock-and-roll badasses. Courtney Love and Lindsay Lohan, though? Those bitches are crazy.

So, as the trainwrecks keep floating up through our social-media timelines and gossip-blog feeds, as the social media pile-ons and hate-reads keep on coming, as this year's girl continually arises, scandalizes, flames out, and is replaced, it's hard to avoid the conclusion that we have a vast and insatiable appetite for specifically female ruin and suffering. And if you, like me, have a tendency toward more-than-mild paranoia involving The Patriarchy, it's hard to avoid the fact that this appetite has reached unprecedented levels right at the moment when women are making unprecedented gains in terms of access, visibility, and general empowerment to enter public life. All those MILEY CYRUS HOSPITALIZED: DID DEATH OF DOG TRIGGER TAILSPIN? headlines were running right next to predictions of Hillary Clinton's presidential candidacy in 2016.

• • •

As long as there has *been* a public sphere, there have been women attempting to *enter* the public sphere, and usually being punished for it. The one thing that all trainwrecks have in common is the temerity to be heard. Where we now exhibit "celebrity meltdowns" on *TMZ*, we used to exhibit "hysterics" on public viewing days at mental institutions. Where we now have sex bloggers living in fear that their real identities will be revealed behind their pseudonyms, we used to have women posing as men or assuming anonymity to publish groundbreaking novels. Where we now have conservative blogs ranting about Clinton's lesbian affairs and/or murder sprees, we used to have poems run in conservative newspapers about how Mary Wollstonecraft— yes, her, the *Vindication of the Rights of Woman* lady—was a suicidal hooker with a shame-baby.

Women who have succeeded too well at becoming visible have always been penalized vigilantly and forcefully, and turned into spectacles. And this, I would argue, is a none-too-veiled attempt to push women back into the places we've designated as "theirs." If you stay at home, get married right away, never get a job, never display any unwelcome emotions, and stay away from the public eye to such an extent that you actually never make any sort of impression whatsoever, you can't become a trainwreck. You become a miserable, sheltered woman living in a prison of her own making, but hey: At least no one's going to disapprove.

But, if you don't plan on doing that, the trainwreck—in

all her varied and historical iterations—is actually a useful figure, in more than one way. She's not just the worst-case scenario. She's not just the cost of showing the world the wrong things, or of being Visible While Female. She's a signpost pointing to what "wrong" is, which boundaries we're currently placing on femininity, which stories we'll allow women to have. She's the girl who breaks the rules of the game and gets punished, which means that she's actually the best indication of which game we're playing, and what the rules are. And, in her consistent violation of the accepted social codes—her ability to shock, to horrify, to upset, to draw down loud and powerful condemnation—she is a tremendously powerful force of cultural subversion. At the end of the day, despite all our praise of strong women and selfless activists and lean-inners, the trainwreck might turn out to be the most potent and perennial feminist icon of them all.

Consider this book, then, a feminist anatomy of the trainwreck. It's an effort to figure out who she is: what her crimes are, why she's making us so angry; what, in general, she hath done to offend us. These are questions of more immediate and personal relevance than you might think: When women look hard enough at the trainwreck, we almost invariably end up looking at ourselves.

So this is an attempt to figure out what we're looking at, and why we keep staring into this particular warped mirror. It is also an attempt to reclaim the trainwreck, not only as the voice for every part of womanhood we'd prefer to keep quiet, but also as a girl who routinely colors outside the lines of her sexist society. It is, above all, an attempt to use the figure of the trainwreck, and our fascination with her, for good: to take all that earth-shattering and civilization-angering power of hers and channel it toward something that might make the world a more just place for the women who live in it.

Part I

THE TRAINWRECK: HER CRIMES

1

SEX

There's no neat and simple taxonomy of the trainwreck. She doesn't come in different flavors, like a bag of assorted lollipops; we don't get a Trainwreck (var. Whore), Trainwreck (var. Drunk) or Trainwreck (var. General Offensiveness). Instead, her sins tend to be messy and boundaryless, to bleed together and become indistinguishable from one another. Once she's found guilty, she's always guilty of more than one thing. But if you want to figure out how and why these women piss off the American public, well, there is one big, obvious starting point.

So let's start here: Who's the first person you imagine when you hear the phrase "celebrity trainwreck"? Summon her in your mind, whoever she is for you: "Wild," out of control, doomed. The girl gone off the rails. Put a name to her, and a face, and hold her in your mind's eye for a minute.

Okay. Second question: Have you seen her naked?

• • •

In my many years of covering gender issues, I have come to perhaps one firm and unshakable conclusion: We, as a society, will never run out of opinions on twenty-something girls' genitalia.

Throughout the 2000s, Britney Spears's vagina was covered by the media as if it were suspected of holding WMDs. It was blogged about, talked about, photographed, and discussed and debated on talk radio and TV: You really couldn't get away from the damn thing. Especially not if you were Britney Spears. The vagina's doings (and, peripherally, those of the woman who owned the vagina, whose sole and exclusive rights to disclose information about it had long since been stolen) were so widely assumed to be a matter of public interest that, when paparazzi caught Spears giving oral sex to her soon-to-be-husband Kevin Federline on a hotel balcony, outlets like *Gawker* and *Salon* linked to the resulting photos.

In *Gawker*'s case, those photos were captioned with pure contempt: "Can we *please* have one fucking day away from Britney, Kevin, and paparazzi photographs that absolutely cannot be allowed to pass without comment?" The writer, charmingly, went on to speculate that the blow job had been arranged by Federline "taping some Cheetos to [his] penis."

So, to reiterate: Someone followed a woman to her hotel, then waited in a concealed location, watching her, until she began to have sex, then photographed the sex, then promptly sold the photos to a public outlet, causing the press to then rebroadcast those photos, while explaining they had no choice in the matter, and making sure to add a link to the appropriate porn site so that the full invasion of privacy could be accessed by their readers. And somehow, in this whole chain of stalking, bad decision-making, and borderline sexual assault, the person who wound up getting the *harshest* condemnation was the woman who'd done nothing but have sex with her boyfriend.

But then, our presumed right of access to young women's bodies extends far beyond Britney. (We'll get back to her later.) In fact, she may not even be the most famous example.

In 2004, Britney Spears was one of the two most-Googled people on Earth. The other was Paris Hilton. Hilton's sex tape, one of the first links posted by *Gawker*'s porn satellite *Fleshbot*, made her infamous; it also received a 2005 AVN award for "Best Selling Title of the Year." This happened despite the fact that Hilton described the sex as, essentially, rape—she alleged that Rick Salomon "forced her to have sex when she was nearly unconscious"; Salomon sued her for defamation—and did not approve of the tape's release. Her supposed promiscuity became so ingrained in her public image that *South Park* dedicated an episode to her:

The fictional Hilton opened a store called Stupid Spoiled Whore, attempted to convert the little girls of *South Park* to her own "whore" lifestyle, and was portrayed, in the immortal words of Wikipedia, as "continuously cough[ing] up semen."

"It annoys me that so many people assume something about me because I had a boyfriend who betrayed me," she said, in a *GQ* interview with Piers Morgan. She also described the tape's release as a trauma: "I just went into shock and just went inside and couldn't come out for days. I was so depressed I didn't even want to come back to America."

"Are you good in bed?" was Morgan's follow-up question. "I guess it's a rhetorical question because I watched the video this morning for research purposes and the answer is clearly affirmative."

It goes on. Spears, Hilton, Lindsay Lohan, and a seventeen-year-old Miley Cyrus were all caught up in the wave of enthusiasm for "upskirts," a strange practice in which grown men with cameras crouched at waist level near celebrity car doors in the hope of documenting whether the women therein wore underpants. Some, it turned out, did not. Again, the results were covered by the national media and/or posted on *Gawker* (sample comment: "What is with these twenty-something girls and their flappy labia?") and again, despite the non-consensual nature of the exposure, the women were the ones to be shamed for it.

Which is not to say that consent has no bearing on how we treat young women's nudity. It has a very real impact. Even if you live in an environment where people are constantly trying to expose your body against your will, and even if those people consistently call you disgusting for being successfully assaulted, you can still make your reputation *far* worse by getting naked voluntarily.

The accusation most frequently aimed at Hilton to justify our treatment of her—and, later, at her former assistant, Kim Kardashian—was that she had intentionally leaked the sex tape. Similarly, women caught in the "upskirt" phenomena were typically accused of seeking attention. To this day, Rihanna can trigger op-eds on the downfall of Western civilization just by showing a nipple. But let's go from the macro-level to the micro, for a moment, and consider the strange fate of Miley Cyrus—tasked, through the holy offices of the Disney Channel, with representing the eternal purity of Heterosexual American Girlhood. There were quite a few major problems inherent in saddling Cyrus with this job, which we'll get to later, but one of the first is that Cyrus did not show any tremendous fondness for "purity"—at least, not to the extent that "purity" can be measured by wearing clothes when in public.

Cyrus is no stranger to sexual-assault-by-press-corps, most of which took place when she was underage. (In addition to the 2012 "upskirt," in 2008, hacker Josh Holly—

going, as fate would have it, by the name "TrainReq"—
stole and posted Cyrus's wet-T-shirt selfies. The photos were
taken when she was fourteen.) Yet this is a mere footnote in
the vast history of Miley Cyrus Sexual Outrage, nearly all
of which was generated by *intentionally* showing up in less
clothing than people expected.

There were rumblings early on, when she posed for a
back-exposing Annie Liebowitz shoot in *Vanity Fair* at the
age of fifteen. ("For Miley Cyrus to be a 'good girl' is now a
business decision for her," her boss, the president of entertainment for the Disney Channel, pronounced ominously.
"Parents have invested in her a godliness. If she violates
that trust, she won't get it back.") In those days, people
tended to claim that their revulsion stemmed from the fact
that Cyrus was too young to be sexualized, and, indeed,
it's demonstrably not a good idea for adults to encourage
minors to take their tops off in photos. Yet that very concern caused people to see everything Cyrus did as sexual:
When she held onto a pole on a moving platform during
one dance, there were op-eds about her "pole dancing." If
she danced in a leotard, wore a short skirt, had a visible bra
underneath her shirt, or touched her torso during a concert, she made headlines.

"It's wrong for Miley to have agreed to play the child
and teen character, *Hannah Montana*, for another year if she
intended to behave like a stripper on stage," blogger Bon-
nie Fuller wrote at *Hollywood Life* in 2010 (headline: MILEY

CYRUS IS AN OVERSEXED TRAINWRECK WAITING TO HAP-PEN!), adding: "She's behaving like the devil."

And so, the very fact that adults wanted to "protect" teens from being seen in a sexual light somehow turned an actual teenager into a stripper, the devil, and the walking embodiment of predatory lust. In 2013, when a twenty-year-old Cyrus twerked against Robin Thicke at that VMAs performance—a mildly risqué move that wouldn't have been very far out of place in *Dirty Dancing*—America reacted as if they'd watched Cyrus personally steal Thicke's marriage certificate and set it on fire. When Thicke and his wife did in fact separate, *TMZ* posted a blaring all-caps headline explicitly blaming Cyrus for the divorce: SPLIT TRIGGERED BY ANTICS WITH MILEY.

There was no affair, no offstage news to report; the "antics" were just the dance, and the fact that Thicke hadn't recoiled and pushed Cyrus bodily away from him into the crowd. Again, Cyrus was solely to blame, for acts which had somehow escalated from scandalous to criminal: In *The New York Times*, Jon Caramanica referred to her "molesting of Robin Thicke," and in Thicke's *Vanity Fair* interview after the event, interviewer Lisa Robinson opened with "Miley Cyrus practically molested you last night at the VMAs."

It wasn't the worst thing she was accused of. Not one, but *two* articles published in 2013 blamed Cyrus for actual, non-metaphorical rape cases. Richard Cohen of *The*

Washington Post wrote that "[Cyrus] is a cheap act, no doubt about it, but for me her performance was an opportunity to discuss one of the summer's most arresting pieces of journalism—a long *New Yorker* account of what became known as the Steubenville Rape." While this is a remarkably flexible definition of the word "opportunity," Cohen's conclusion bears noting: Cyrus's existence, apparently, "encourages a teenage culture that has set the women's movement back on its heels." Soon enough, Joanne Bamberger at *USA Today* chimed in: "I was ready to dismiss the 'let's condemn Miley' parade, until I read a story about a Montana man convicted of the statutory rape of a fourteen-year-old student in 2008 . . . it doesn't seem to be a huge leap to suggest that with young girls increasingly sexualized in the media, teen victims of sexual assault may be judged more harshly because too many see a child as being 'in control.'"

Cyrus's response to all this has been, if anything, to lean into the trainwreck. For every theft of naked photos, she gets aggressively more naked; for every complaint about her bad behavior, she gets more ill-behaved. It's hard to remember, in all the noise, but the Miley Cyrus of her "adult" records—the star who flashes her bare breasts at awards shows, poses for full-frontal nude photos in magazines, and talks continuously not only about the fact that she uses recreational drugs, but about which drugs she's using—is not so much an attempt to "provoke" our outrage, but the only logical response to the outrage that has always surrounded her. We told this child, throughout her teenage years, that her naked body, her drug use, and her outrageous behavior were the only interesting things about her, and that we would steal that information if it wasn't promptly forthcoming. Now, Miley is both literally and figuratively stripped down, naked and yelling about getting high on live TV ("Yeah, I smoke pot" is an actual Miley Cyrus lyric), with nothing left to hide and nothing more for us to steal. And our response has been to tell her to cover up, and to reminisce about what a sweet little girl she used to be before it all went wrong.

A victim turns into a perpetrator; a naked body that people were willing to commit theft to see becomes unsightly and shameful the moment it's exposed consensually. Sexually pure or sexual predator, uncorrupted virgin or corrupting whore, godly or Godzilla: These are the options. Thus are trainwrecks made.

All of this matters, for reasons beyond the enduring grossness of gossip blogs. Public sexuality is the first, and maybe the primary, mark of a trainwreck, whether her sexuality is forcibly exposed or consensually shared. This is not an accident: It's a very public working-out of a long-held myth about heterosexual sex.

Men (well, straight men—but in this version of the myth, all men are straight—sorry, fellas) supposedly react to women's sexuality the way my dog reacts whenever I eat a slice of pepperoni pizza: total, unhinged, uncontrollable urge to seize and devour. They want it, they need it, and they can't be held accountable for what they do to get it, whether that's staring and begging, or stealing it when your back is turned. (And for "stealing," read: leaking nudes, groping, or rape.) Yet most people believe that society would not benefit if the world were to devolve into one long, public orgy. Men want sex—all the time, and with everyone—but they can't be allowed to have all the sex they want. So, with half the world barely able to restrain themselves from whipping it out on the subway platform, someone has to keep us all from wrecking our marriages and dry-humping each other in the streets. And this group (surprise) is women.

As continually as men pursue sex, women are asked to refuse it. We're the responsible parties, who hold the pizza above the dog's head, where he can't get to it. If we are good women (or "good girls," to quote the infantilizing terminology of many occasionally Robin-Thicke-centric pop songs) we utilize sexuality only strategically, and only in the service of tricking men into getting married and fathering children. We are also paranoid and crafty enough to prevent anyone from "stealing" it when we refuse. We're responsible, not for taking care of our own bodies and lives, but for keeping society intact.

Once you've made women's sexuality a load-bearing

structure for the social order, the obligations only proliferate. Soon, she finds herself not only responsible for tricking men into fatherhood, but for keeping the right team in charge as regards heterosexuality (consider how Lindsay Lohan's downward reputation spiral was hastened by the fact that she dated a woman), race (how many jokes have you heard about Kim Kardashian dating black men?), class (a big complaint about Britney and K-Fed was not just that they had sex, but that they looked like "white trash" together), and anything else you can think up.

The responsibility also hits women differently depending on where they stand in the social hierarchy. Surveying the grand tradition of Trainwreck Journalism, it's hard not to conclude that it's vastly overpopulated with young, pretty, blond white women. It's not that society places some especially low value on white blondes; quite the opposite. All of the aforementioned ideals about sexual purity were constructed with white women in mind. Therefore, we treat their sexuality as an exception to the rule, a personal failing. Black women, on the other hand, have already been stereotyped as hypersexual and "impure," and from them the same behavior draws not personal condemnation, but generalized racism; not shock or horror, but contempt. It doesn't spare these women any unkindness, and it's no more rational than the alternative— Taylor Swift and Beyoncé can both wear leotards and talk about their feminism at concerts, but only Beyoncé will

have the leotard cited as a reason she can't be feminist—
but it changes the angle from which we bring the hammer
down.

And, where white women are slapped down for daring
to be sexual, women of color are slapped down for daring
to be anything *else*: Over the course of her career, Nicki Minaj has spoken about abortion rights, the need for female
musicians to write their own work, the difficulty of being
an assertive woman in a business setting, and the obstacles
black women face in being recognized as creative forces.
She is the best-selling female rapper of all time, and her success has done a tremendous amount to awaken critical and
commercial interest in female voices within a genre that was
largely seen (fairly or unfairly) as a man's game before she
showed up. Nicki Minaj has done everything in her power
to frame herself as a thoughtful black feminist voice, up
to and including staging public readings of Maya Angelou
poems. And yet, approximately 89 percent of Nicki Minaj's
press coverage, outside the feminist blogosphere, tends to
focus on: her butt.

The Nicki Minaj Butt Conversation—whether she has
had plastic surgery to enhance her butt, whether there is a
sufficient amount of clothing apportioned to her butt, what
her butt means for society, and/or for our own personal
butts—has been louder and longer than common sense
would seem to allow. "Nicki Minaj Butt" has its own search-
able tag on the *Huffington Post* (sample headline: J. LO'S BUTT

TAKES A BACKSEAT). Elsewhere, entertainment news and gossip sites are strewn with highbrow, intellectually stimulating headlines like NICKI MINAJ'S BUTT EXPOSED IN SHEER JUMPSUIT DURING DUBLIN CONCERT, and EVEN NICKI MINAJ ISN'T SURE IF HER BUTT IS PHOTOSHOPPED OR NOT, and NICKI MINAJ BUTT IMPLANT RUMORS ARE TRUE!, and finally, depressingly, NICKI MINAJ FIRES BACK AT HATERS WHO SAY HER BUTT IS THE REASON SHE'S FAMOUS.

Nicki Minaj's butt is perfectly fine, of course. She seems to have a healthy relationship with it; she's rapped about it from time to time. But given the abundance of other accomplishments and qualities we could be talking about, it's starting to feel as if Nicki Minaj could solve the mysteries of cold fusion and still be seen largely as (in the words of one popular YouTube parody) "a stripper who also knows how to rap."

Similarly, heterosexuality—the grand structure underpinning all these freak-outs—is the "norm." It's assumed, until it isn't. But when a woman is presumed to be heterosexual, it normally takes exposed skin to trigger public freak-outs, invasions of privacy, and media handwringing. When a woman is rumored to be queer—a rumor that tends to arise whenever the press has trouble placing a famous woman with an equally famous man—all it takes is for her to go outside in the company of another woman. Whitney Houston's close relationship with her childhood friend, Robyn Crawford, was so widely examined and whispered about that, partly in order to defeat the rumors, Houston rushed into a marriage with Bobby Brown. Which, of course, did wonders for her happiness and reputation.

And, as our understanding of gender and sexuality gets deeper and more complicated, we seem to keep finding new reasons to shout at people. It was only in 2015, after a good eight or nine years of being shamed for being insufficiently feminine and/or a "bad example" of girlhood, that Miley Cyrus made it clear that she is not a girl. She identifies, roughly, as "gender fluid," somewhere between and beyond the male-female binary. She's also not straight; "I don't relate to being boy or girl, and I don't have to have my partner relate to boy or girl," she's said. One hopes that the world will be kind. But, considering the innumerable crude jokes and accusations of Ruining Feminism Forever that transgender celebrities like Caitlyn Jenner and Laverne Cox have had to endure, it's not hard to predict that the next wave of Miley Cyrus Sexual Outrage is just beginning.

The reason for this is what it always has been: A woman who's "out of control" sexually isn't just a person making decisions, most of which will never affect you. She's a defector from the ongoing sexual warfare; her influence stands to tear the whole system down.

•

Anatomy of a Trainwreck

MARY WOLLSTONECRAFT

She was a concubine. An adultress. A prostitute. She sold herself to "half the town." She was a "usurping bitch," with "much amiss in the head," an "unsexed," genderless "maniac" with "no sense of guilt," "whom no decorum checked." Her work, if allowed to spread, would pervert young women's minds and destroy their innocence; it was a "scripture, archly framed, for propagating whores."

Today, Mary Wollstonecraft is so respectable that she's actually not intrinsically interesting. She's an eighteenth-century feminist, well-entrenched in the canon, whose *Vindication of the Rights of Woman* is a staple in any Women's Studies student's list of Books You Should Probably Get Around To, I Mean, Not Now, But Eventually. Her points have been so widely accepted that they neither shock nor enlighten: education for women? Sure! Women voting? Why the heck not? Letting ladies be doctors? Yes, yes, very good. Let's move on to the hard stuff.

So you wouldn't guess that for most of the time Wollstonecraft has been a part of the canon, she was known pri-

marily for her scandalous sex life. Nor would you know that
while she may have written the first book of Western feminist theory, she was also the trainwreck that functionally
derailed the feminist movement for one hundred years.

In her lifetime—a brief one; she was born in 1759, and
died in 1797—Wollstonecraft was respected. She was connected with the writers and theorists of the British far-left
wing; when people thought of her, they thought of French
revolutionaries and pro-democracy radicals like Thomas
Paine. Granted, "armed revolution against the monarchy"
was not exactly a mainstream position. But it did have quite
a lot of traction, particularly in France and the newly established United States, and Wollstonecraft enjoyed a surprising amount of legitimacy as a result.

Vindication was well situated in a debate people were already having over the concept of "natural rights," which
kept it from seeming foolish, and made it one of those
books that people felt obliged to know, if only so that they
could argue about it. John and Abigail Adams read her work
carefully. Aaron Burr (himself not the most well-liked guy
in history) had a portrait of Wollstonecraft over his man-
tel, and educated his daughter according to Wollstonecraft's
theories. The conservative *Anti-Jacobin Review*, in one of its
many takedowns, quipped, "*Rights of Woman*, which the superficial fancied to be profound, and the profound knew to
be superficial"—but even they were forced to admit that
people were listening.

And then she died. Quickly, unexpectedly, and early, at the age of thirty-eight. She had the great misfortune to have, at that time, an adoring husband, the philosopher William Godwin, who was determined that her genius should be remembered. He arranged for the publication of all her remaining work (including, fatally, her letters), and took the eight weeks immediately after her death to write a biography, *Memoirs of the Author of the Vindication of the Rights of Woman.* To this day, it's hard to say why Godwin did what he did: It could have been political conviction, or the hazy judgment of fresh grief, or simply the inability to understand that anyone might dislike the woman he'd loved. But for whatever reason, in his biography, William Godwin set out to expose every damaging secret Wollstonecraft ever had. Most crucially, he exposed the importance of two names: Henry Fuseli and Gilbert Imlay.

Fuseli was the lesser offense. He was a self-consciously risqué painter, with whom Wollstonecraft had gotten involved just as he was getting married to one of his models. This culminated in a spectacularly awkward episode in which Wollstonecraft arrived at Fuseli's doorstep, asked his horrified wife for permission to move in, and was thrown out on her face. In 1798, this story alone would have been enough to destroy a woman's reputation. But, as it turns out, it was just an opener for the main event, featuring the American writer, father of Wollstonecraft's first child, and All-Time Great Historical Douchebucket, Gilbert Imlay.

Wollstonecraft and Imlay lived together in France, where she had gone to cover the Revolution. This was at the height of the Reign of Terror, when saying the wrong word in the street could result in execution; England had declared war on France. So, to avoid Wollstonecraft's being taken for a British spy, they claimed to be married. The idea, though, was to be *better* than married: Like many radicals of the day, they believed in a higher bond, something outside of the patriarchal arrangements, which could be held together by love rather than legal consequences. Or at least, they believed it for a time. Then, Wollstonecraft gave birth to their daughter, Fanny. At this point, *she* believed in a higher bond, and *he* believed he had to go out for the proverbial pack of cigarettes—you know, not far out, just *out*, preferably across a national border or an ocean or two. Be back soon! Love you, honey! Bye!

It would have been cruel to simply disappear, but what Imlay did was crueler: For months, Wollstonecraft wrote to him, begging him to return, only to be put off each time with promises that he'd rejoin her as soon as his "business prospects" allowed. She believed him for longer than sense would seem to permit. But then, there was very little that made sense about her situation. She was a woman with a newborn, living in a war zone, and the person she most trusted kept telling her that the truth she could almost certainly perceive—she was alone, she was unprotected, Fanny had no father—was a delusion brought on by her own overheated emotions. Unmoored and gaslit, her tone became steadily darker. She began to mention death more often. She wrote that she could not sleep. That she wondered if she were already dying. "I wish one moment that I had never heard of the cruelties that have been practised here, and the next envy the mothers who have been killed with their children," she wrote. "You will think me mad: I would I were so, that I could forget my misery—so that my head or heart would be still."

Finally, in April of 1795, Wollstonecraft arrived in London and discovered what had kept Imlay: While she'd been fearing death, raising their baby and begging for his return, he had been living comfortably in London with another woman. Strung-out, overwhelmed, and at the end of her tolerance, Wollstonecraft attempted suicide with a laudanum overdose.

Imlay, to give him credit, personally rescued her from the attempt. Imlay, to give him less credit, somehow convinced her to hide herself *again*, assuring her of her importance and then sending her away to Scandinavia. She went, wrote a book about it—one of her more well-received works, in fact—and returned to find Imlay still with his new partner. She tried to drown herself in the Thames. This time, she told Imlay not to save her: "Nothing but my extreme stupidity could have rendered me blind so long," she wrote to him. "Yet, whilst you assured me that you had no attachment, I thought we might still have lived together . . .

Your treatment has thrown my mind into a state of chaos; yet I am serene. I go to find comfort, and my only fear is, that my poor body will be insulted by an endeavour to recall my hated existence."

But, once again, she survived. And, in time, she got down to the business of surviving; she cared for Fanny, she returned to work, she found a way to be alone. "I flinch not from the duties which tie me to life," she was able to write to Imlay, in late 1795. And though the angry letters about the deterioration of their relationship and the fate of their child continued until about 1796, she was happy to report that when she saw him in the street, she could say hello without experiencing any strong feelings whatsoever.

By that time, of course, much of her focus was on her old friend, William Godwin. As she recovered, the friendship had quickly turned romantic, and sexual (another fact Godwin was all too eager to share with the world), and in 1797, when Wollstonecraft once again found herself pregnant, they bit the bullet, overcame the years in which both of them had publicly fulminated against marriage as an institution, and officially got married.

William Godwin and Mary Wollstonecraft had only been married for six months when she died from complications of childbirth. His state of mind is probably reflected in the name of their daughter: Simply "Mary Wollstonecraft." (Later to be known as Mary Wollstonecraft Godwin, and even later, of course, as Mary Shelley.) He claimed that he had fallen in love with her through her writing. He had just committed to spend the rest of his life with her. And then, almost overnight, she was gone. In the midst of his grief, Godwin did something that he believed would keep Mary's name alive.

Godwin published the old suicide note. He published Wollstonecraft's tender recollections of sex. He published the bitter breakup letters in which Wollstonecraft told Imlay that he was a sex-crazed, loveless asshole who would turn into a sad old man. All of it, everything: It was out there. And it was attached to a woman who had argued, of all things, that emancipating women would make them *more virtuous*.

So, that was the tragedy. And here were the reviews:

> *William hath penn'd a waggon-load of stuff*
> *And Mary's life at last he needs must write,*
> *Thinking her whoredoms were not known enough,*
> *Till fairly printed off in black and white.*
> *With wondrous glee and pride this simple wight*
> *Her brothel feats of wantonness set down.*
> *Being her spouse, he tells, with huge delight*
> *How oft she cuckolded the silly clown*
> *And lent, O lovely piece! Herself to half the town.*

That was the *Anti-Jacobin* (they're the folks responsible for the "scripture" line, along with timeless zingers such as "God help poor silly men from such usurping bitches.") There was also this, from Richard Polwhele, concerned with the damage wrought by "unsex'd females" like "WOLLSTONECRAFT, whom no decorum checks":

> *Come, from those livid limbs withdraw your gaze,*
> *Those limbs which Virtue views in mute amaze;*
> *Nor deem, that Genius lends a veil, to hide*
> *The dire apostate, the fell suicide.*

And this, from Robert Browning, who took it upon himself to write a poem in the voice of Mary Wollstonecraft herself, and whose "Mary Wollstonecraft" is, essentially, a blithering idiot with a stalker's crush (she has "more than a will—what seems a power / to pounce on my prey") who pretends to be smart in the vain hope of getting a boy to notice her:

> *Much amiss in the head, Dear,*
> *I toil at a language, tax my brain*
> *Attempting to draw—the scratches here!*
> *I play, play, practise and all in vain:*
> *But for you—if my triumph brought you pride,*
> *I would grapple with Greek Plays till I died*[.]

It's not quite "Stupid Spoiled Whore," but it's close. (The main difference, I would argue, is that it leaves out the

"Spoiled" bit.) Wollstonecraft's promiscuity and craziness ballooned outward from the facts, becoming monstrous. The *Anti-Jacobin* implied that we'd only heard about two instances of Wollstonecraft having premarital sex because Godwin was intentionally leaving out hundreds of others: "The biographer does not mention many of her amours. Indeed it is unnecessary; two or three instances of action often decide a character as well as a thousand."

The dates on these things are particularly illuminating. The *Memoirs* and the letters were released in 1798, shortly after Wollstonecraft's death. Polwhele wrote his immortal verse in 1798, too, and the *Anti-Jacobin* was still cackling about Wollstonecraft's "whoredom" in 1801. But Browning's thoughts on Wollstonecraft's desperation and stupidity went out in 1883—eighty-five years after the scandal first hit. Godwin's *Memoir* didn't affect Wollstonecraft's reputation, it *was* her reputation, more or less until the dawn of the twentieth century.

As Wollstonecraft went, so went her cause. When *Vindication* was first published, it seemed that women's rights would be naturally folded into the discussion of human rights, part and parcel of the increasing democratization of culture. But after the *Memoirs*, they dropped out of view: Even her former employer, the *Analytical Review*, was forced to conclude that some people "will be apt to say, that the experience of

Mrs. G is the best refutation of her theory." Another magazine was more to the point: "Her works will be read with
disgust by every female who has any pretensions to delicacy;
with detestation by everyone attached to the interests of religion and morality, and with indignation by anyone who
might feel regard for the unhappy woman, whose frailties
should have been buried in oblivion."

And bury her they did. The progressives who used to
read her, such as John Stuart Mill, increasingly either avoided
the topic of feminism or carefully eliminated all mention
of Wollstonecraft when framing it. Novelists writing for
lady audiences filled their plots with misguided, sex-crazed
feminists who threw themselves at men—or off cliffs. The
prediction that her work would be read with particular revulsion by "females" was correct; it was women, in fact,
who increasingly drove the shaming of Wollstonecraft, in
an effort to avoid being associated with her disgrace. In
1885, socialist Karl Pearson proposed naming his activist
group after her. It was the women in the group who threatened to resign. Even if you believed in the brotherhood and
equality of all mankind, you didn't want to march into battle
calling yourselves the Crazy Slut Fan Club.

The only way for a woman to engage in feminism at
all, it turned out, was to actively participate in the shaming:
Harriet Martineau, one of the few to carry the torch, declared that "Mary Wollstonecraft was, with all her powers, a
poor victim of passion, with no control over her own peace,

and no calmness or content except when the needs of her individual nature were satisfied." Not only were *real* feminists entirely unlike Mary Wollstonecraft, allowing women like her into the movement set it back: "[Their] advocacy of Woman's cause becomes mere detriment, precisely in proportion to their personal reasons for unhappiness, unless they have fortitude enough [. . .] to get their own troubles under their feet, and leave them out of the account in stating the state of their sex."

A whore, a madwoman, an idiot, a joke, and most of all, responsible for setting women's rights back. It didn't matter that she'd started the conversation about their rights in the first place. Feminism was for women who behaved correctly and had their shit together. As for Mary: Mary was over. She was wrecked.

•

The leap from Paris Hilton to Mary Wollstonecraft may seem like a long one. But in practice, it's hardly even a bunny hop. The pattern of forcible exposure and public shaming that governs female sexuality is very old, and has changed very, very little. We simply find new personalities and new technologies with which to recreate the same drama.

In the summer of 2014, Eron Gjoni published "thezoepost," a 9,000-word blog post. It was perhaps the world's most exhaustive and lamentable effort on the part of an ex-boyfriend to prove that his girlfriend—well-reviewed

feminist game developer Zoe Quinn—was a bad person.
It was also, if you watched closely, an eerie play-by-play re-
enactment of the furor surrounding Wollstonecraft and the
Memoirs.

"This post exists to warn you to be cautious of Zoe,"
Gjoni began. "It is here to paint a portrait of her actual
personality."

That "actual personality," in Gjoni's view, was entirely
comprised of the fact that, during their five-month relationship and/or the three months they'd been broken up, Quinn
had slept with other people. Gjoni knew the language of
left-wing and feminist outrage well enough to mimic it effectively ("I *very* much align with SJ [social justice]," he assured *Vice*) by claiming that his post was "helping a very
large number of abuse survivors" and taking care to "apologize to those [. . .] who have been triggered."

Yet despite the highflown rhetoric, Gjoni's definition of
"abuse" was highly unorthodox—specifically: It failed to include his own behavior. Gjoni posted chatlogs in which he
interrogated and browbeat Quinn into messy, borderline-
suicidal breakdowns by calling her a liar and telling her that
she was exactly like her violent mother and ex-husband. He
counted as one of her sins the fact that she'd refused to let
him search her private message archives for the word "love."
At one point, he even started calling hotels for "evidence"
that she'd been there with other men.

About those hotel calls: Those, actually, were not in

Gjoni's original post. He wrote about them on *4Chan*, one of the most powerful and virulent sources of online harassment for women, where Gjoni went to rally support for himself. He also posted the entire contents of "thezoepost" to *Something Awful* and *Penny Arcade*; Quinn alleged, when she filed her restraining order, that Gjoni knew them to be primary sources of previous harassment.

Still: He published it. He published the Facebook message in which she wrote "I should kill myself." He published the fact that one of her partners had been married. He published her pleading with him not to tell that man's wife to "go public" with the affair. In 2014, as in 1798, it was enough to burn a woman down to the ground.

Where Godwin's disclosures were motivated by foolish love, Gjoni's came from knowing and calculated hate. (He would casually admit on Twitter that he calculated the odds of Quinn being harassed at 80 percent when he published.) But both had the advantage of cultural momentum: The communities Gjoni courted were already powerfully angry at "SJWs" ("Social Justice Warriors," or, generally, leftist women) and feminists who criticized their beloved videogames. They leapt at the chance to take their anger out on one of these women, under the premise that she'd been immoral. These men quickly proceeded from crowing about Gjoni's post, to concluding that Quinn's career was entirely due to sexual favors, to (of course) leaking nude photos she'd taken and/or posting her address online, to, finally, theorizing the existence of a vast feminist conspiracy to destroy video games as we know them.

Gjoni's gesture was vile, but it was also silly: It was overwrought interpersonal drama from a small subculture (independent video game developers) that the mainstream rarely thought about, let alone tracked. But, as with Wollstonecraft's disgrace, the chance to publish something embarrassing about a feminist woman, and therefore to discredit feminism itself, was an opportunity that got right-wing types salivating. One of the primary exponents of GamerGate, as the phenomenon came to be known, was Milo Yiannopolous, a "journalist" ensconced in the far-right hive mind of Breitbart.com, who published dispatches from the movement with titles like "Feminist Bullies Are Tearing the Gaming Industry Apart," eagerly repeating apocryphal charges that Quinn "cheated on her boyfriend for calculated professional advancement" with men who "know that they will be rewarded with sexual favours for promoting substandard work by some female developers."

And so Gjoni's Gjrudge Match leapt past the bounds of the subculture, into the deep waters of general far-right sexual outrage. Quinn began to receive a torrent of rape and death threats: "Next time she shows up at a conference we . . . give her a crippling injury that's never going to fully heal . . . a good solid injury to the knees. I'd say a brain damage, but we don't want to make it so she ends up too retarded to fear us," ran one threat, quoted in *The New Yorker.* Other long-standing female targets of the "gamer" community, including Anita Sarkeesian and Brianna Wu, began to receive credible death threats and cancel their public appearances. If a publication criticized "GamerGate," its advertising sponsors soon received waves of threats and harassment that sometimes caused them to withdraw support from the publication. And even this wasn't the worst manifestation of the backlash: Several of GamerGate's enemies, including web developer Israel Galvez, strayed GamerGater Grace Lynn, and critic Randi Harper, were subject to "SWATing," a uniquely horrific tactic in which harassers reported false incidents to the police and gave their victims' address as the source, thereby causing armed SWAT teams to show up at the target's door. Developer Caroline Sinders, another target, was not SWATed herself—but SWAT teams were sent to threaten her mother.

It would be tempting to conclude that society is moving away from the hysteria and unprocessed, raw sexism that defined the upskirt-crazed, sex-tape-centric turn of the century: When dozens of female celebrities had their private nude photos leaked in 2014, the response was largely angry and concerned for the women in question, rather than gleeful, with sites like *Jezebel* (a *Gawker* property) and *Salon* joining with victims like Jennifer Lawrence in calling it "a sex crime." Twenty-three U.S. states have laws against revenge porn—the non-consensual leaking of sexual tapes or photos—and Google will now remove it from search results at the victims' request. As my colleague Amanda Hess wrote, declaring the death of the celebrity sex tape, "the Internet masses [have] found a new vice, outrage, to replace our voyeurism."

Not so fast. For one thing, outrage and voyeurism have never been distinct vices. The trainwreck lies straight in the center of the Venn diagram where the two overlap, converting hatred, anger, and scorn into an almost hypnotic fascination with the subject, an inability to look away from her, and an increasing need to see her exposed.

In fact, sex scandals are marvelous for their ability to turn the realities of prurience into the language of high-flown morality or pseudo-progressive politics. Watching Hilton's video, as Hess herself writes, was framed as a form of "class warfare," a way to "knock the princess down a peg." Making a TV episode that depicted the victim of a sex crime as constantly gagging on semen was more acceptable if you first took the trouble to call her "spoiled."

Similarly, the cruelest commentary aimed at trainwrecks often takes on a veil of pro-woman, pro-girl righteousness. The revulsion at Cyrus's real or (mostly) perceived sexuality was consistently framed in terms of high-toned objection to rape culture; Cyrus was accused of either "molesting" male pop stars or of giving actual child molesters ideas. The *Daily*

Mail can justify calling Rihanna a "whore" in a headline by claiming that her videos' "crudity and dancing, combined with money-focused lyrics, are telling Rihanna's fans— many of them still children—that it is good for women and girls to sell their body." One might even call them a scripture for propagating whores.

It's not all trumped-up dudgeon, either. As with Wollstonecraft's exile, even genuinely feminist women can participate in the cycle. Consider feminist Elinor Burkett, taking to the pages of *The New York Times* to kick Caitlyn Jenner out of cisgender feminism's lunch table, citing Jenner's "idea of a woman: a cleavage-boosting corset, sultry poses, thick mascara and the prospect of regular 'girls' nights' of banter about hair and makeup." It ostensibly meant to reclaim feminist purity from mainstream beauty standards, but it sure did sound like she was calling Jenner a slut.

At times, leftist sexual critique and conservative prudery can be nearly identical. When Milo Yiannopolous mocked Beyoncé's self-identification as a feminist in the UK *Independent*, declaring that "sexual titillation for men [is] . . . perhaps the least effective route to female empowerment imaginable" and calling Beyoncé "what men demand of her, less than the sum of her body parts," it was hard to tell him apart from the feminist *Ms.* readers who were offended by the magazine's Beyoncé endorsement, and who swarmed its Facebook page to complain about her "wearing these stripper outfits onstage while dancing like a stripper all for men."

The nasty but unavoidable truth is that political outrage and the good old-fashioned desire to punish "bad" women are not disconnected. The field for one has been fertilized (or, if you prefer, salted) by the other. Complex, deep, and necessary critiques—like the feminist critique of mainstream beauty standards, in Jenner's or Beyoncé's case, or the critique of class privilege, in Hilton's case, or the anti-racist critique of Cyrus's appropriation of black aesthetics and the industry's simultaneous dismissal of black artists (Nicki Minaj wound up having to make a few)—are appropriated and imitated by the mainstream to rationalize our culture's underlying pattern of demolishing sexually unruly women. And even socially conscious women (myself very much included, I must admit) can easily fall into age-old and socially encouraged habits of punishing sinners, unaware of which patterns have taken hold until it's too late. Exposure and punishment, sexual transgression and murderous rage: The cycle holds, from the eighteenth century to the twenty-first. We keep women's bodies controlled, and women themselves in fear, with the public immolation of any sexual person who is or seems feminine, keeping even "private" women inhibited by reminding them of the catastrophe that will ensue if they live out their desires too freely.

Good-girl-gone-queer Lindsay Lohan, divorced single mother Britney Spears, Caitlyn Jenner with her sultry poses,

Kim Kardashian having the gall to show up on the cover of *Vogue* with her black husband: All of them are tied to the tracks and gleefully run over, less for what they've done than for the threat they pose to the idea that female sexuality fits within a familiar and safe pattern. If control over women's bodies were the sole point of the trainwreck, that would be terrifying enough. But it's only the beginning: Shame and fear are used to police pretty much every aspect of being female. After you've told someone what to do with her body, you need to tell her what to do with her mind.

2

NEED

The sex in the Wollstonecraft (or GamerGate) scandal was only half the story. The story of a woman happily fucking her way across the world stage would, no doubt, enrage a large portion of the population. But half the point of creating a villainess is being able to witness her downfall. It's in the breakdown—the messy, pleading letters, the self-loathing chat transcript, the suicide attempt, the broken relationship, the vision of a woman being punished with total emotional collapse—that the appeal of the trainwreck narrative really lies.

The big sales pitch for ideals of feminine purity, after all, is that they make women happy. If a woman keeps it together and plays by the rules, she supposedly gains safety, approval, love, and the glowing sense of well-being that only comes from not being chased down the street by people who think she's an unholy bitch. If a woman strays from the path, however, she pays for it. And not just because we

make her. Her lack of virtue makes her unlovable and cor-
rodes her from within.

The truthfulness of this is, well—what's the most po-
lite way to say this?—horseshit. There are plenty of well-
behaved women living lives of quiet desperation, just as
there are no doubt plenty of reckless women having the
time of their lives. But trainwreck narratives seize on the
stories that serve the sales pitch: the one where the bad girl
gets hurt in the end.

If sex is one of the easiest ways for a woman to invite
hatred and mockery in our culture—to be labeled a slut, a deviant, or any one of the many unprintable slurs that we use to
mean "transgender woman"—then ceasing to have sex with
someone should be a reliable solution to the problem. And
yet, it is not so. Breakups, you see, lead to sadness, and also
to anger. And, instead of admitting that women feel unpleasant emotions when they're in unpleasant situations, we have
a tendency to label any public display as bitter, vindictive, ob-
sessive, pathetic, desperate or, yes, "crazy."

If there were any one woman who could elude the media's
hunger for celebrity carnage through sheer force of good
behavior, it would be Taylor Swift, the woman *PopEater* once
crowned "The Teen Anti–'Train Wreck.'"

Swift's persona played perfectly to the ideals of feminine
purity and innocence that her unlucky peers had been caught

violating. The press marveled that her lyrics were "wholly unlike the banal sexual come-ons that crowd the music of most of her contemporaries." She did everything right and took all the right stances: against casual sex ("Where's the romance? Where's the magic in that? I'm just not that girl"), against revealing costumes (" 'I wouldn't wear tiny amounts of clothing in my real life so I don't think it's necessary to wear that stuff in photo-shoots"), against sexting (her phone contained only text messages; "You wouldn't find any naked pictures"), against premarital virginity loss (one single, "Fifteen," bemoaned the fate of a friend who "gave everything she had to a boy who changed his mind"). She did not drink, did not use drugs, and told interviewers her idea of fun was spending time with her parents. Just to drive the point home, a few of Swift's songs pitted her against overtly sexual harlots—"Better Than Revenge" concerned "an actress / [who's] better known for the things that she does on the mattress"—whom Swift demolished with the sheer rhetorical force of her righteousness.

Swift's image struck some as sanctimonious, or at least, a little too dependent on trashing other women. But it worked: The CEO of her record label, Scott Borchetta, crowed to *The New York Times* that "[Swift] isn't a person who's going to wake up half-naked, drunk in a car somewhere in Hollywood"; Swift herself took to *Seventeen* magazine to "defend her good girl image": "Honestly, if somebody wants to criticize me for not being a trainwreck, that's fine with me!"

Nothing gold can stay, Ponyboy. No matter how well behaved Swift was, she couldn't avoid the non-stop, invasive media coverage that comes with her level of celebrity, and the public indignities that are its more-or-less invariable result. One of the key selling points for Swift, in that "Teen Anti–'Train wreck'" piece, ran as follows: "She's never really been tabloid fodder—we don't know who she dates."

That . . . well, that changed. By 2014, thanks to a few high-profile relationships and a few breakup songs, most of Swift's album press was devoted to figuring out which song was about which boyfriend. And most of Swift's media and/or songwriting strategy was focused on convincing the world that she was not "some clingy, insane, desperate girlfriend." *TMZ*'s head honcho, Harvey Levin, had released a video calling her a "nutcase" and "BATBLEEP CRAZY." Levin made his point with his typical subtlety; the video's title on YouTube was "Taylor Swift—HAS SHE LOST HER MIND?!?" Still, the allegation resonated even among writers with a healthier relationship to the caps-lock key. *Thought Catalog* ran a piece entitled "Taylor Swift Is a Psycho"; *The Frisky* provided a list of "Seven Crazy Taylor Swift Girlfriend Moves"; *DListed* responded to the news that her latest single was about a breakup by dubbing her the "Bad Seed of music" and a "crazy bitch."

The allegation was always the same: Taylor Swift dated men, and got dumped by men, specifically so that she could write cruel songs about them and harm their careers:

"[Swift's] career depends on her getting laid and having her heart broken," wrote Ryan O'Connell in the *Thought Catalog* piece. "That's what 99 percent of her songs are about. If we don't know who she's sleeping with, what else is there to really know about her?"

The coverage, slowly but inevitably, turned inside-out, until she was receiving the exact inverse of the praise she'd gotten for having no visible love life. Even if you had been a Swift skeptic, this was bizarre. She had written and performed breakup ballads since the start of her career; in this, she was much like every musician to step within twenty yards of a microphone. But the same behaviors that had gotten critics and moral guardians gushing in 2009 were, by 2012 at the latest, considered to be symptoms of lunacy and promiscuity. She'd played the game exactly right, and she still hadn't won it—not completely, not without incurring penalties. Which is what happens, when games are designed so that no one can win.

If Swift has been cast as the scary, angry Psycho Ex—out on a rampage of peppy, blond, Max-Martin-enabled revenge—at least she can thank her lucky stars that she's not Jennifer Aniston. (*Star Magazine* report on Taylor Swift, 2014: "Why can't I keep a guy? I feel like I'm turning into Jennifer Aniston.") Aniston, once crowned "America's Favorite Spinster," has spent ten years and counting stuck on the pathetic-and-needy end of the spectrum.

Following her 2004 divorce from Brad Pitt, Aniston reportedly became so desperate for the touch of a man that she drained his very life force: In 2008, *CelebrityFix* warned us that "the ex-*Friends* star has a habit of being a bit too much in relationships—a characteristic that pissed off her ex-husband Brad Pitt," and that "she's back to her 'clingy' ways now that things are getting serious with new man John Mayer." Once the saintly Mayer had managed to extricate himself from Aniston's iron grip, she reportedly went about looking for new men to throttle: In 2011, *Hollywood Life* reported that "Jennifer Aniston's latest romance with actor and writer Justin Theroux may be over almost as quickly as it started," and that Theroux was "already complaining how Jen is suffocating him."

Aniston and Theroux got married. But this has done nothing to cure Aniston's essential dumped-ness, nor slow her descent into madness: "Jennifer Aniston is apparently suffering from PTSD," warns *Celeb Dirty Laundry* in 2014. "It seems she can't be reminded that Angelina Jolie and Brad Pitt exist without some sort of dramatic episode." The site goes on to relate one such "dramatic" incident, in which Aniston attended a party where the hosts were showing *Mr. & Mrs. Smith*—the movie on which Pitt and Jolie reportedly began dating—and . . . well, "and" nothing. *CDL* notes that Aniston "ultimately tried to act as if it were no big thing," no doubt restraining her natural impulse to throw herself through a window.

Of course, these gossip sites are just trying to manufacture a story that will interest their readers. No one is going to click on a headline that reads JENNIFER ANISTON WENT TO A PARTY AND NOTHING MUCH HAPPENED, after all. But it's still instructive to note who the story is about. No one is writing blog posts about the massive relational trauma of Brad Pitt; it's women, specifically, that we like to see disintegrating or overreacting.

Plenty of men get rejected by their partners. Plenty of men react in over-the-top, unflattering, or just plain dangerous ways to that rejection. Eighty-seven percent of stalkers are male, and, in the case of specifically female victims, 62 percent are former husbands or boyfriends. In 2008, 45 percent of all female murder victims were killed by a partner, as compared to 4.98 percent of male victims. In a terrifyingly high number of cases, women's ex-boyfriends have turned out to be Eron Gjoni. (Well, okay, there's only one of him. Still, it should terrify all of us that he's still walking around, free to ask women out on dates—and that there are other men out there who are just as frightening.) Yet not all the *4Chan*-based temper tantrums and filed restraining orders in the world have been enough to make "crazy ex-boyfriend" a pervasive stereotype.

In fact, men are remarkably free to be publicly sad and lonely. It's romantic: Think of Lloyd Dobler in *Say Anything*, parked outside of his ex-girlfriend's house with his boom box hoisted high. We see those men as fragile, sensitive, or wounded. We don't see them as crazy. Yet the most well-

known movie about a woman who stands outside a former lover's house and refuses to leave is *Fatal Attraction*, in
which the female lead's stubborn romantic longing quickly
escalates into home invasions and/or murdering the house-
hold pets.

And this legacy gets handed down to the rest of us civilians, for whom the Crazy Girlfriend—the girl who calls too
much, texts too much, cries too hard, gets too angry, takes
revenge, holds a torch, won't let go—is the subject of countless advice columns and listicles. Everyone knows the character, in one way or another. Men are counseled on how to
avoid her. Women are counseled on how to avoid being her.

On *xoJane*, for example, you can find the by-now-
notorious piece "I Slept With a Crazy Woman," in which the
male writer details his horrifying encounter with a woman
who did such insane things as (a) text him, (b) drink, (c) text
him while drinking, and, finally, this: "Crazy D asked if I
wanted her to blow me again. It felt like an odd move—too
much, too soon and slightly desperate. Who blows someone
twice on the first date, I thought." So add "too sexually gen-
erous" to the list of crazy-woman signifiers—although that
shouldn't be too surprising.

The association of emotional instability and sexual
openness—"crazy in the head, crazy in the bed," to quote
an old proverb of the Bro-American community—is no
accident. The crime of a slut is physical, and the crime of
the crazy girlfriend is emotional, but both are crimes of

overabundance; the rules against being "crazy" are more or less the same as the rules against being "slutty," played out on another, deeper level of control.

The other half of desire is wanting to *be* desired—wanting other people to find you attractive, or fascinating, or likable, so that you can have the amount and kind of sex you really want. In some instances, desire is wanting to be loved. Naturally, if your society is already stomping out female desire on the level of sheer physical impulse, this weightier, more personal need—to be actually important, in the eyes of at least one other person; to be seen as good, and valuable, and worth listening to and respecting—is even more taboo. A woman who wants you to love her is dangerously close to becoming a woman who demands the world's attention. Whether your girlfriend wants you to stop going to strip clubs or stop passing legislation that bars her access to safe and legal abortion, the scary thing is that she's started *wanting* things, and you might have to actually do them. The relationship is not one-sided any more. She's started acting as if she can write the rules.

In an ideal patriarchal world, men pursue relationships, create relationships, and end relationships; women simply sit there and get related to, answering male desire and affection rather than feeling their own. "Crazy" women, again, are women who operate as subjects rather than objects, women who want things rather than passively accept the fact of being wanted; they're seen as unnatural and grotesque because their desire exists on its own terms, rather than in answer to male needs.

So the ultimate clarifier is to ask, not what constitutes "crazy," but how surreal and artificial a perfect rendition of "sane" heterosexual romance would look on these terms, and what a woman would be if she were genuinely only activated by male desire rather than her own: A woman who imitates a man's affection levels seamlessly, instantly, like a reflection moving in a mirror. She reaches out when he reaches out; leans in when he leans in; declares love when he declares love, wants sex when he wants sex, backs away when he backs away. When he leaves, she disappears.

It's when she doesn't leave the frame, when she moves in ways men don't prompt or expect, that a woman unsettles us. She stops being a reflection, and becomes a presence: A person, suddenly standing in the room.

•

Anatomy of a Trainwreck

CHARLOTTE BRONTË

The story begins, as all things must, with a timid governess. A woman in her twenties—not particularly pretty, not particularly wealthy, socially awkward—sets out into the world, determined to earn her way by gainful and ladylike employment. The education and moral uplift of the young, perhaps: This would allow her to live an independent and sufficient existence, while performing acts pleasing unto her God.

Stop me if you've heard this one before. Or don't, actually, because this is where it gets interesting. This particular young woman is, unbeknownst to everyone including herself, about to write some of the best-known and most widely beloved books of the nineteenth century. This entirely unexceptional young woman would not draw our notice, were it not for the very exceptional fact that she is Charlotte Brontë.

It's not that Charlotte lacked ambition. All of the Brontës were bookish children, and they began to write at an early age. They collaborated on a family magazine, which summed up the highlights of their life together, and wrote not one but two epic, sprawling fantasy sagas: Branwell and Charlotte, the older children, had created the world of "Angria," and Anne and Emily, within a few years, followed suit by creating "Gondal." So Charlotte knew that she could write, and she knew that she loved writing, and naturally, as she grew older, she wondered if she could turn it into a career.

But the response she received was chilling. When she wrote to the poet Robert Southey for advice, telling him she wanted "to be for ever known" as a poet, he informed her that, while she undeniably had some talent, it was irrelevant: "Literature cannot be the business of a woman's life: & it ought not to be. The more she is engaged in her proper duties, the less leisure she will have for it, even as an accomplishment & a recreation. To those duties you have not yet been called, and when you are you will be less eager for celebrity."

It's not merely Southey's "advice" that is depressing, but the eager, obsequious tone of Charlotte's response. "I had not ventured to hope for such a reply," she wrote, "so considerate in its tone, so noble in its spirit. I must suppress what I feel, or you will think me foolishly enthusiastic." To assure him of her virtue, she went on to outline the womanly "duties" currently on her plate: "My father is a clergyman, of limited though competent income . . . I thought it therefore my duty, when I left school, to become a governess," she wrote. "In that capacity I find enough to occupy my thoughts all day long, and my head and hands too, without having even a moment's time for one dream of the imagination. In the evenings, I confess, I do think, but I never trouble anyone else with my thoughts."

I confess, I do think. Here was a woman seeking to establish herself as a writer, while being required by her male contemporaries to keep so busy with her proper feminine tasks—marriage, housekeeping, and, most importantly, the rearing of children, whether they were her own or someone else's—that she didn't have the time or inclination to sit down and imagine anything, let alone to develop those thoughts into a substantial piece of writing. To seek publication was, by definition, to "trouble" other people with her thoughts. To publish would mean that she had failed at being female.

And then, there was the question of money. Jane Austen had been able to write her novels under conditions that, while certainly not ideal—she took up a small table in the family sitting room, covering her work with a sheet of paper when someone interrupted her to make conversation—also involved full days spent at home, and a guaranteed lifetime income from her family. But when Charlotte told Southey that she scarcely had time to think, she was telling the truth: She was a governess in a private home: a combination nanny, teacher, and all-around workhorse. The job was miserable—at one point, the children pelted her with rocks until she bled—and, understandably, did not last long. And, when it ended, she set out with her sister Emily to teach at a Belgian girls' school. It was here that she met the school's owners: Madame Claire Zoe et Monsieur Constantin Heger.

We still don't know precisely what happened with Constantin. In fact, it's remarkably hard to even understand why it happened. Photographs reveal a short, severe-looking middle-aged man, with a receding hairline and the sort of craggy, unforgiving features you'd expect to see on someone waving a shotgun full of rock salt and telling you to get off his lawn. His personality wasn't any more appealing than his looks: "He is professor of rhetoric, a man of power as to mind, but very choleric and irritable in temperament," is how Charlotte first describes Heger, in a letter to her friend Ellen Nussey. She also describes him as an "insane tom-cat" and a "delirious hyena," and mentions that he frequently reduces her to tears. Fredericka McDonald, another teacher at the school who later wrote a book about the Heger-Brontë affair, was a bit nicer, crediting Heger with "intellectual superiority, an imperious temper, a good deal of impatience against stupidity, and very little patience with his fellow-creatures generally." She, too, noted, that "M. Heger liked his pupils to cry, when he said disagreeable things." It was apparently the only way to stop him from saying them.

What it came down to, in the end, was that Charlotte was lonely. Emily went back to England. Charlotte scarcely spoke French; she couldn't talk to anyone. She found the Belgians cold and unfriendly. She tried to distract herself by wandering the streets, just to get the sense that she was part of a crowd, but it didn't work. The language was different, the culture was different. Even the religion was different: Charlotte, the daughter of a Protestant curate, got so desperate for emotional support that she wandered into a Catholic church and made confession, a lapse in piety for which she never quite forgave herself. And then, there was the fact of her age; she was twenty-six, and she had never published a piece of writing, fallen in love, or worked at a job she did not hate.

"My youth is leaving me," she told a friend, who'd suggested she might try working as a nurse. "I can never do better than I have done, and I have done nothing yet."

Finally, it all got so bad that Charlotte tried to quit the school, just started to walk out of the building with the intention of never coming back. But someone stopped her. One person, in all of this, told Charlotte Brontë that she had value, and persuaded her to stick around. That someone was Constantin Heger.

There was something else about Constantin that people tended to notice, something outside of his forbidding looks and nasty temper. He became a different person—a warm, charismatic, irresistible person—when he wanted to teach you something. Here's Fredericka again: "The funny and pleasant thing about M. Heger was that he was so fond of teaching, and so truly in his element when he began it, that his temper became sweet at once; and I loved his face when it got the look upon it that came in lesson-hours: so that, whereas we were hating each other when we crossed the threshold of the door, we liked each other very much when we sat down to the table; and I had an excited feeling that he was going to make me understand."

We don't know whether Charlotte Brontë and Constantin Heger had an affair. We don't know whether he loved her, whether he seduced her, whether he even so much as flirted with her; whether it was a forbidden romance or simply a misguided, one-sided crush. But what we do know is that Constantin Heger was Charlotte Brontë's writing teacher. He made her write essays for him in French, to improve her grasp of the language. He critiqued the essays, in depth, and passionately. He praised her skill. He made her read books—gave her books as gifts, many times—and spoke with her about what she read. Some people even believe she may have spoken to him about her earlier attempts at writing, may have gone so far as to show him pieces of the Angria stories. There's no evidence of a sexual affair, but there's every evidence of a passionate textual affair, and in those moments, the blessing of being taken seriously as a reader and writer must, almost certainly, have blended with that strange, funny, exciting charm that Constantin possessed only when he wanted to teach you something. For the rest of Charlotte Brontë's life, Constantin Heger and the act of writing were inextricably linked.

"Do you know what I would do, Monsieur?" Charlotte once wrote to Constantin, in a letter discussing her career plans. "I would write a book and I would dedicate it to my literature master—to the only master I have ever had—to you, Monsieur . . . That cannot be—a literary career is closed to me—only that of teaching is open[.]"

So I'm asking you: Imagine that. Imagine being a female genius, trapped in the nineteenth century, trapped in a job you hate, in a country not your own. You have some of the best books of your age inside you, and you've resigned yourself to the fact that you'll probably never get them out, never do anything better than those stories you used to make up with Anne and Emily back home. You're teaching kids, and that's the only thing you'll ever do, because even if you did write—even if you *did*—decent women don't publish their writing. It's unladylike, it's unfeminine, it's vulgar, it's condemned. It's a distraction from the business of a woman's life. You have no escape. And you have no hope. All you have is one man—one short, bald, mean, angry, middle-aged, married man—who sits down with you to work on your writing. And in that moment, when he's speaking to you about books, there is no one who could not love his face.

Imagine how much you'd love that man's face, if you were Charlotte Brontë. Imagine that man's power: all the needs he would fulfill, all the desires he'd awaken, all the lives you'd suddenly realize you could be living.

And imagine it well, because you're going to have to forgive Charlotte for some truly crazy ex-girlfriend behavior once she went back to England.

> *July 24, 1844: I have been told that you are working too hard and your health has deteriorated a little—That is why I refrain from uttering a single complaint about your long silence—I would rather remain six months without hearing from you than add an atom to the burden . . .*

> *October 24, 1844: I would just like to ask you whether you heard from me at the beginning of May and then in the month of August? For all those six months I have been expecting a letter from you, Monsieur—six months*

of waiting—That is a very long time indeed! Neverthe-less I am not complaining . . .

January 8, 1845: *I did my utmost not to cry not to complain . . . I do not seek to justify myself, I submit to all kinds of reproaches—all I know—is that I can-not—that I will not resign myself to the total loss of my master's friendship—I would rather undergo the greatest bodily pains than have my heart constantly lac-erated by searing regrets. If my master withdraws his friendship from me entirely I shall be absolutely with-out hope—if he gives me a little friendship—a very little—I shall be content—happy, I would have a mo-tive for living, for working . . . I don't want to reread this letter—I am sending it as I have written it—Nevertheless I am as it were dimly aware that there are some cold and rational people who would say on reading it—"she is raving" . . .*

November 18, 1845: *I have done everything, I have sought occupations, I have absolutely forbidden myself the pleasure of speaking about you—even to Emily, but I have not been able to overcome either my regrets or my im-patience—and that is truly humiliating—not to be able to get mastery over one's own thoughts . . . Your last letter has sustained me—has nourished me for six months—now I need another and you will give it me—not be-*

cause you have any friendship for me—you cannot have
much—but because you have a compassionate soul . . .
To forbid me to write you, to refuse to reply to me—that
will be to tear from me the only joy I have on earth—to
deprive me of my last remaining privilege—a privilege
which I will never consent to renounce voluntarily.

Of their correspondence, only these four letters survive. None
was supposed to: Even these four were torn up by Heger and
thrown into the garbage. (His wife fished them out and sewed
the fragments back together. And—just to add a little more
fuel to the speculative fire—at least one biographer would
later swear she'd done this because Charlotte Brontë blamed
Madame Heger for making her leave the school, and that,
as Charlotte was leaving their house for the final time, she
turned to her and muttered the words *"Je me vengerai." I will be*
avenged.) But the pattern is clear: Every letter gets a little bit
louder, a little bit needier, a little bit sloppier, a little bit more
desperate. In every letter, she reaches a higher and higher
pitch of emotion. It's with this final letter of November 18—
the one where she insists, she demands, she rages, she tells
him flat-out that she will never stop writing to him, never
stop begging him to write back—that she appears to lose him
entirely, after two years of pleading. This is where it ends.

Except that it doesn't end. Almost exactly two years
later, in October 1847, a man named Currer Bell publishes
a novel entitled *Jane Eyre*, about a timid yet ardent governess

who falls for her unhappily married employer. It is very successful. It is also very, very scandalous. One reviewer decries its "truly offensive and sensual spirit." When her publisher's mother accidentally leaves a copy lying around the house, visitors scold her for leaving *Jane Eyre* within reach of children. Honestly, if this governess is such a good girl, what's she doing, making eyes at the boss? And what's he doing, making eyes back?

Meanwhile, in the literary world, people are asking a different set of questions. No one's ever met this "Currer Bell" guy. No one has any evidence that he exists. It's a pen name, clearly, but whose? Whoever it is, he's not very sneaky: There's an "Acton Bell" and an "Ellis Bell" being foisted on the public, and they could not more obviously be the same person. (In fact, they were Anne and Emily Brontë, respectively.) Fingers start pointing to William Makepeace Thackeray, the *Vanity Fair* author, whose wife—it's well known—went crazy, tried to drown herself, and had to be shut up somewhere in Paris, a few years back. He's been praising *Jane Eyre* to the skies, told an editor he had to miss a deadline because he couldn't stop reading it. Obviously, this is Thackeray, trying to sneak out an account of his own marriage by using a fake name.

Other people have an even wilder theory. They think "Currer Bell" might actually be a woman: Thackeray's mistress, some governess he took up with after the wife fell apart. Maybe Thackeray taught her to write. Maybe Thackeray taught her to write a book about what it's like to have an affair with Thackeray. Some people dismiss this out of hand, as being patently ridiculous—no woman could have written *Jane Eyre*; there's sex, there's violence, there are curse words, for goodness sakes'—but the suspicion, once planted, keeps growing. It would explain everything: the fake name, the dirty content, the general air of secrecy. *Jane Eyre* is obviously the work of a fallen woman, the dissolute and corrupted mistress of some married man.

When Ellen asks her about her connection to the *Jane Eyre* scandal, Charlotte Brontë denies everything: "Whoever has said it—if any one has, which I doubt—is no friend of mine. Though twenty books were ascribed to me, I should own none." To her publisher, she writes panicked letters about the desperate importance of making sure that her cover isn't blown, that she is always and only referred to by her pen name. If anyone gets a whiff of who she is, she says, "I should deem it a misfortune—a very great one."

Oh, and one other thing: Prior to *Jane Eyre*, Currer Bell had been shopping a different novel, one which was rejected by every publishing house that saw it. The title of that first book was *The Professor.*

Do you know what I would do, Monsieur?

•

As I say: There's something perversely liberating in this story. Or in reading the Heger letters themselves: long, rambling, increasingly sloppy and hyperbolic and out-of-control. You can read the same descent into tearful begging and desperation in Mary Wollstonecraft's letters to Gilbert Imlay.

In both cases, these women are desperate—but not in any trivial or stereotypical way. We spend so much time pathologizing "overemotional" women that we scarcely ever ask what those women are emotional about. Here, it's clear: Both women are, in different ways, in fear for their lives. In Wollstonecraft's case, there is the physical threat of living inside a bloody and anarchic war, and the difficulty of providing a decent life for her daughter as a social outcast; in Brontë's case, there is the psychological danger of being buried alive, of the demands of daily feminine life slowly eroding her intellect until there is nothing left. Both women are drowning, and they hold onto the men in their lives with the desperate, superhuman grip of a shipwreck survivor clinging to the side of a lifeboat. It doesn't look pretty. But then, survival in a desperate situation never does.

And even if it doesn't: Who cares? Ugly as these relationships may have been, human relationships, or the need to be loved, can look (and feel) a whole lot worse than this.

There are relationships that are, yes, crazy: co-dependent, or abusive, or just plain toxic. But the cult of the Crazy Ex-Girlfriend does very little to keep these relationships from happening, let alone to educate people about how they work.

Think of all the times high-profile rape or abuse cases are framed as the acts of "vindictive" women, looking for revenge or a financial pay-off from the men who've dumped them; think of the Julian Assange rape case, during which Naomi Wolf accused the two women who'd pressed charges of using the "dating police" to punish Assange for not becoming their boyfriend. Think about Anita Hill, reporting that Clarence Thomas had sexually harassed her, and the infamous line of questioning pursued by Senator Howell Heflin: "Are you a scorned woman?" he asked. And: "Do you have a martyr complex?" Meanwhile, lawyer John Doggett testified that Hill was delusional, afflicted by "erotomania"; his evidence was a possibly fabricated story about how she had once accused him of "leading her on" after he canceled a date.

All of this falls under the heading of what lawyers call the "nuts and sluts" defense. When women report men's sexual misconduct, the standard tactic of a defense attorney is to discredit those women by painting them as either sexually promiscuous, afflicted by an excess of desire, or "unstable" and vindictive, driven to hurt men because they can't control their own emotions. Sexual overabundance or emotional overabundance: Either one renders you less than a victim in the eyes of a jury.

When we live in a climate of distrusting women's voices, of viewing women as primarily obliged to service the relationship demands of men, their pain—pain that goes beyond hurt feelings or loneliness, pain that comes from actual abuse—is always suspect. We can blame them for not being good, not making their male partners happy. We can say, not that abuse has made them act angrily or strangely, but that they were abused because they were angry or strange. And this is true even when the abuse in question is incontrovertible and well documented.

Not only do we make trainwrecks out of abuse victims, abuse has added to the ignominy of many of the most famous cases. Think of Whitney Houston, found bloodied at the site of a domestic-violence call. Think of Amy Winehouse, seen running into the street and pleading for help from passing cars, with a bruise in the shape of a man's hand on her throat.

Winehouse was open about the fact that she would die for Blake Fielder-Civil, the husband who introduced her to crack and heroin, and from whom she fled on the night in question. (When questioned, she covered for him, claiming that she was misbehaving and he "saved her life.") At one point, a reporter who'd wandered into her house at 4:00 a.m. recorded Winehouse telling a friend that, if she'd ever really been in love, "you'd be dead because you weren't together." Fielder-Civil was in prison for charges related to an armed robbery by that time, and Winehouse was in fact a few years away from death. But that didn't stop anyone from turning her shout-outs to "my Blake, incarcerated" into a running joke.

Similarly, when Rihanna was beaten by her then-boyfriend Chris Brown in 2009, the fact of the abuse, and its severity, were factually established—photos of her bloodied face were leaked to the press. But, almost overnight, urban legends about what Rihanna had done to "provoke" Brown sprang up on the Internet. She had given him an STD! She had thrown his car keys through a window! A "Rihanna Deserved It" T-shirt was sold on CafePress. And in one survey of two hundred teenagers, 46 percent blamed Rihanna for the assault. The line of logic speaks for itself. Here's a sample, from *Yahoo! Answers*:

> *Im a women myself and I never want to get beat by a man, but I know if I ever do he's going to be beating me for a good damn reason . . . suppose Rihanna was just going crazy and was hitting him, Im sure he could have shaked her or something but still, I know as a women sometimes we can get a little crazy with emotion*[.]

Yet, when Rihanna reconciled with Brown—"I decided it was more important for me to be happy . . . even if it's a mistake, it's my mistake," she said at the time—she was hated for that, too, with an onslaught of blog posts labeling her a "bad role model" and a traitor to women everywhere. "Gone [are] the days where women and everyone around the globe praised her for leaving the destructive and violent relationship [she] had been in with Brown," celebrity blog *Tell Tales* claimed, ignoring the fact that "everyone around the globe" absolutely had not done that. "Today, Rihanna is letting down her fans and friends by accepting the R&B artist back in her life." *HollywoodLife* accused her of "telling young people everywhere that domestic abuse is healthy" and sending a "toxic message"; they quoted a self-help author who claimed that "She's setting a terrible example because we know there is a high amount of abuse in teenage and adolescent relationships. They are going to follow her lead."

Yes, dating Chris Brown was a bad idea. But this is strikingly unfair. Rihanna was called crazy for leaving Chris Brown, and called crazy for staying with him; there was no way out of the condemnation, no matter which route she took, and the actual abusive man in question was let off the hook for his choices in both scenarios. Rather than Chris Brown having a responsibility not to abuse women, it was always Rihanna's responsibility not to *be* abused—and, no matter what she did, she was always blamed for any abuse that did or could happen.

The strange thing is, relationships like hers don't go against the script about the woman who only exists to be related to, who disappears the moment a man isn't interested: They're a literal and faithful read. The romantic trope of the woman who only cares about her boyfriend and the horror-movie trope of the woman who only cares about her ex-boyfriend are more or less the same woman; she becomes wonderful or terrible depending on how the man in question feels about her. But that same script doesn't give a woman any excuses for walking away. She's supposed to stay until he's done with her and die (or at least commit to invisibility) when he leaves. And it turns out that, when she does just that, she's also turned into a punch line.

Simply because we've been taught to value men's voices over and above women's, our natural response to a woman's claims of violence is to see her as delusional (she can't perceive the real story) or unstable (she can't handle the real story) or just plain frightening (she knows the real story, but she's out to get him). Which means that a tremendous number of female stories—perhaps the most urgent and enlightening ones, the stories we most need to hear—have been shut down or silenced. Or it means that women have silenced themselves, believing that if they ever truly admitted what they were going through, they would sound crazy.

She did come out eventually, Charlotte. She let people know that she was a woman. She even let people know which woman she was; attended parties (Thackeray hosted a few), became a part of the literary scene. She waited until her sisters Anne and Emily had died, and eventually wrote a preface, letting people know their names, and how much she had loved them, and the conditions of their lives.

"We did not like to declare ourselves women, because—without at that time suspecting that our mode of writing and thinking was not what is called 'feminine'—we had a vague impression that authoresses are liable to be looked on with prejudice," wrote the woman who'd once been told that literature could never be a woman's profession. "We had noticed how critics sometimes use for their chastisement the weapon of personality, and for their reward, a flattery, which is not true praise."

It was then, nearly ten years into her career, that Charlotte Brontë published her final novel, *Villette*. It was the account of a young woman named Lucy—not particularly pretty, not particularly wealthy, socially awkward—who is forced to make her way by teaching at a girls' school in a French-speaking country much like Belgium. She hates it there. She's lonely, isolated, so desperate that she goes into a Catholic church and makes confession, a sin in piety she cannot forgive herself. But, at this school, she meets a professor—a short, ugly, angry man; a man of power as to mind, but very choleric and irritable in temperament—and they fall in love. Notwithstanding the interference of the vile headmistress, an evil woman who wants the professor all to herself, he loves her back, wholeheartedly, and they are engaged to be wed. Nevertheless, they are separated, when he must go across the sea. And yet, Brontë writes, the separation of this young woman and her adored professor does have one consolation:

> *By every vessel he wrote; he wrote as he gave and he loved,*
> *in full-handed, full-hearted plenitude. He wrote because*

he liked to write; he did not abridge, because he liked not to abridge. He sat down, he took pen and paper, because he loved Lucy and had much to say to her; because he was faithful and thoughtful, tender and true.

Well: Constantin didn't write. He didn't seem to give or love much, either. He was neither faithful nor thoughtful, not tender and not true. And he brought Charlotte Brontë to her knees.

But when she finally gave up on the hope that he might write to her, something else began. Something far more important. We all know how *Jane Eyre* ends: *Reader, I married him,* etc. But what most people miss is the fact that the most important word of that sentence is not "married." The real payoff comes far earlier. It feels so natural that most people miss it entirely. They don't realize that it was the most impossible part of the sentence to imagine, or to achieve. So consider the triumph—the sheer, improbable triumph—in that one word. In the fact that, after everything that was torn up, tossed in the garbage, frozen out, laughed at, lectured against, she still got you. Look past him, married, look past *I.* Look to yourself: *Reader.*

3

MADNESS

When I was twelve years old, I concocted a plan to win over the cool kids at my school by having the coolest, funniest Halloween costume at their party. Other girls were going as witches, or kitty cats. Boys would be zombies—a little fake blood, it was easy. Not me. I wanted to get creative with my monster.

I wanted to be Courtney Love.

Courtney was the bête noire of our suburban middle school clique. We all loved her husband—Kurt, poor Kurt, dead Kurt, Kurt who had struggled. We all understood that Nirvana was the greatest band that had ever existed. I have a distinct memory of sitting in a boy's bedroom, staring at Kurt's three-foot-tall head on a poster (*MTV Unplugged*, the one where he looked really upset to be there) and hearing the boy murmur, "It's so weird that we got to be alive for him, you know?" Kurt was to be our Christ: We had trod the earth with him, and dipped our hands in his wounds, and would forever more witness his true gospel, untainted by the blasphemies of posers.

But, before you could truly accept Kurt into your heart, you had to get that Courtney Love was Satan. She'd married him to get famous. She'd stolen his songs. She made fun of his suicide note; in fact, some people said, she probably killed him. She was rude, she was mean, she was loud, she said "feminist." She punched people, and at concerts, you could always see her underpants. Sometimes even (we whispered, darkly and with fear) her boobs.

So I got a pink dress and snipped at it with scissors until it was miniskirt length. I put on a pair of boots—I didn't have Doc Martens, but old, scuffed-up winter boots worked—and a blond wig, and I fucked up its hair. I put on makeup: too much of it, and smeared to look wrong. My mother evaluated me to see if the overall look was too provocative ("you don't actually want to be like this woman, do you?" "Mom, nobody wants that, that's the point") and I was out the door.

And then, when I was safely out of my mother's sight, I whipped out my *pièce de résistance*. I took a safety pin, and scraped it down my arms, to give myself track marks. I had no idea what "track marks" were, really: how they got there, what they said about your health, why they were shameful. But I knew Courtney Love had them. And I knew that, because Courtney Love had them, they were funny.

"When Kurt died, I just fell into this endless spiral,"

Courtney Love told addiction and recovery website *The Fix* in 2012. "I was doing drugs from the moment I woke up till the time I went to bed." Her album came out four days after he died. Her bassist overdosed a few months later. She hid in her house—"there were people outside her house every day. People in the trees, people throwing microphones in the yard," a friend said later—and in her first concert, she went through the set sobbing, changing lyrics so that they alluded to her own impending death, and collapsed on stage.

So that was my monster costume. Dressed as a grieving mother whose husband had blown his head off, giving myself track marks to sell the gag. It was cool. It was funny. I was twelve years old.

It's easy to say that you shouldn't despise women for having sex, or getting naked. Nearly everyone has sex, or at least human genitalia that might show up in a photograph. It's also easy to say that you shouldn't punish women for being sad or angry about a failed or abusive relationship, since loss is one of those things that tends to make most humans feel sad. These are crimes that even "nice girls" can commit, albeit inadvertently. It's not hard to rally sympathy to their cause.

But the full trainwreck treatment doesn't begin until you've passed beyond the preliminaries. Check off one or two boxes on the list, and you might come off fine, if slightly worse for wear. The women we truly despise don't just make common mistakes. They aren't flawed in everyday ways; they aren't just whiny, or clingy, or slutty, or loud. These are the true spectacles, the ones we remember, not in incidents, but in images: Amy Winehouse, walking down a London street without her shirt or her shoes. Lindsay Lohan, posing with a butcher knife between her teeth. Amanda Bynes and her tattered Halloween wig, Sinead O'Connor ripping a photo of the Pope in half, Britney hammering at a car with an umbrella. They're where sexual overabundance and emotional overabundance collide and merge into something that is both, and neither, and worse than either. They are addicted, delusional, suicidal, violent; they are mad.

This is a story about images. So flip the pages backward, for the moment—to before gossip blogs, before tabloids, before photography, even—to one painting, done in 1876. It depicts the legendary Paris hospital of La Salpêtrière.

La Salpêtrière was an institution in the heart of Paris that housed women who had gone wrong. It held thousands. Though it was originally intended to be a warehouse for the homeless, in time, more and more women found their way in: They drank too much, or had sexually transmitted diseases. They were developmentally disabled, or epileptic. They were old. They were prostitutes. They saw things, or heard voices, or refused to eat. The crimes were many, in La

Salpêtrière, but the punishment was always the same: Here, in what Georges-Didi Huberman called "the city of incurable women," you were chained to the walls and left to die.

Getting from La Salpêtrière to *TMZ* is a quick trip: We can do it in three doctors and two paintings. Here is Pinel, our first doctor, and the hero of Painting Number One: Tony Robert-Fleury's *Pinel Liberating the Madwomen of La Salpêtrière.* Pinel has bold new ideas about how to run La Salpêtrière. He thinks the chains are a bad idea, for one thing. He thinks these women may be basically rational creatures afflicted by deformations in their thought processes—illnesses of the mind, if you will—that a doctor could resolve by speaking with them.

So Pinel comes to take the chains off the madwomen. Yet the funny thing about Pinel, in Fleury's painting, is that he's hardly visible. You have to look to spot him: a sober, respectable, middle-aged man in a nice suit, so dark he nearly fades into the background. What this image concerns, chiefly, is what he's "liberating": a landscape of writhing, white, exposed female flesh.

One girl, her flimsy white gown slipping down her shoulder to show her cleavage, smiles hazily as men grip her by the arms. An angry-looking woman in a low-cut shirt lunges at the viewer from her knees, mouth agape. Another woman lies on the ground, back arched, gasping. She's torn her gown away to expose one naked breast.

Oh, sure, there are a few old hags around the edges.

Sure, we're meant to focus on what the doctor did. But we all know what we're here to see. These girls—these pretty girls, these crazy girls, unable to control themselves, unable to even keep their clothes on—my, oh, my, how awful. My, oh, my, how shameful.

My, oh, my. Isn't it strange, these crazy girls. You just can't look away.

Fleury's choice to turn a human-rights violation into a soft-porn showcase might be more shocking, were it not for the fact that it was an approved psychiatric practice at the time.

Enter Doctor Number Two.

Pinel Liberating the Madwomen hung in the lecture hall of Jean-Martin Charcot, the neurologist who gave La Salpêtrière its other great historical distinction: as the cradle of "hysteria." The word had been around for quite some time—it was what happened when a woman's uterus got out of place and made her act badly, or when she was sexually frustrated, or when she was too promiscuous; whatever it was, doctors theorized that up to 75 percent of women were afflicted—but Charcot was the first to codify it as a disease of the mind. He even theorized that some men could have it, though it was rare.

But hysteria didn't make much sense, even as a mental illness. Not quite epilepsy, not quite insanity, hysteria was what you had when the doctor didn't know what you had. Women who cried too much had it. Women who laughed too much had it. Women who masturbated at all had it. So did women who disliked sex. Charcot was tasked with bringing clinical specificity to a disease that thrived on not being anything specific. He didn't succeed, of course. But he did have a flair for public relations. And so, to keep the world abreast of this amorphous yet dangerous epidemic, he resorted to photography, bringing his patients into a professional studio so that he could capture them as they screamed, arched, grimaced, and twitched.

Publicly exhibiting the mentally ill was an old practice; beginning in the 1600s, English tourists could pay a penny to visit the cells of chained lunatics at Bedlam. It was supposedly a morally uplifting reminder to restrain one's own animal passions, though according to accounts from the time, most of the visitors were laughing. But, where Bedlam imprisoned men and women alike, Charcot's emphasis on women in peril made him a sensation.

His most famous subject was a fourteen-year-old rape victim named Louise Augustine Gleizes. Louise Augustine was younger, and prettier, than most patients—"the camera likes her," photographer Paul Regnard explained—and Charcot published photographs of her writhing on a bed in her underclothes (these were her "passionate poses": "ecstasy," "amorous supplication," "erotism") accompanied by descriptions of the strange states she fell into under hypnosis. ("She closes her eyes, her physiognomy denoting possession and satisfied desire; her arms are crossed, as if she were clasping the lover of her dreams to her breast; at other times, she clasps the pillow. Then come little cries, smiles, movements of the pelvis, words of desire or encouragement.") All of this was for educational purposes, mind you. Sure, sure. And people visited Bedlam to improve their souls.

In addition to the photography business, Charcot performed his hypnotic treatments publicly, allowing the world to see the power he had over his broken women. Louise Augustine turned in a few performances, but his star in these live shows was Blanche Wittman, "queen of the hysterics"; she could do the most remarkable things under hypnosis, including kissing members of the audience on command. Indeed, there were many remarkable things about Blanche—chief among them the fact that, after Charcot died and the hypnotism sessions ended, she never exhibited another symptom of hysteria for the rest of her life.

Still, despite these little factual infelicities, hysteria was a smashing success. Charcot became the most celebrated doctor in France; he even got his own painting, by Pierre Aristide Andre Brouillet, *A Clinical Lesson at the Salpêtrière* (Painting Number Two). It shows Charcot's handsome male assistant holding Blanche, who is wearing a low-cut gown and opened corset for the performance, and swooning in his arms as if she's posing for the cover of a romance novel. A group of rapt young men crane their necks from the stands, trying to get a good look at all the hot, hot mental-health care going on.

And, just as *Pinel Liberates the Madwomen* hung in the lecture hall of Charcot, a copy of *A Clinical Lesson at the Salpêtrière* hung in the offices of one of Charcot's most devout admirers: Sigmund Freud. Doctor Number Three. Freud felt that Charcot, brilliant though he was, had not done enough to emphasize the sexual causes of hysteria; his own studies were dead-set on unlocking the secret carnal desires of women. Freud could be remarkably insensitive about said desires (Dora, perhaps Freud's most famous patient, relates an incident when an adult man cornered her and forced a kiss on her as a little girl; Dora claims she did not like this; Dora, Freud concludes, is lying about the fact that she did not like this, because Dora is a hysteric; et cetera) and his studies were often, shall we say, suspect in their methods. One woman, who had gone to Freud with leg pain, remembered him only as the "nerve specialist" who "tried to persuade me I was in love with my brother-in-law."

But, like it or not, Charcot was a mere Obi-Wan to Freud's Darth Vader: The student became the master, and the contemporary idea of mental illness took shape in Freud's office, under the watchful cleavage of Blanche Wittman, and inside the long history of broken, exposed and shameful women.

So flip forward. Look at the photos again. Here is a woman unconscious, mouth wide open, head thrown back. Here is a grimacing woman with a shaven head. Here is a woman in a flimsy slip, sobbing, straining against the handcuffs that fasten her to a hospital gurney. Here is a woman starving and half-naked, wandering the street, her face twisted into a rictus. Here is a woman stepping out of a car, her skirt pulled aside to expose her vulva.

Is it starting to look familiar yet? When you envision the tourists at Bedlam, or the demonstrations at La Salpêtrière—the strange, half-dressed girls contorting and flirting, not even in control of their own bodies—can you tell yourself that you'd be too sensitive, too good at heart, to ever find yourself in the stands?

The "hysterics" of Charcot's time, or Freud's, would now get different names: They'd have anorexia, post-traumatic stress disorder, bipolar disorder, borderline personalities.

But no matter what they had, they would still be spectacles. They belong to the visual history of the Madwoman: half-clothed, unhinged, somehow both sexually titillating and fundamentally abhorrent, grotesquely exposed and irresistibly available. Half the time, with "crazy" celebrities, we don't even know what these women's diagnoses are, or whether they have them: Try to prove that Britney Spears has bipolar disorder, or that Amanda Bynes is schizophrenic, and you wind up at a dead end, defeated by doctor-patient confidentiality. Amy Winehouse was undoubtedly an addict. But her emaciated appearance—the source of many, if not most, cruel jokes about how ugly she'd become—was largely due to bulimia, which no one in the media knew she had until years after her death.

But it doesn't matter that we don't have a diagnosis. We already have a name for it; we already know what disease you have when the doctor won't say what disease you have. Add sexual overabundance to emotional overabundance, and throw in an element of danger or death, you have the sum total of what we once called a "hysteric." Now, we call it a "trainwreck." And then, as now, the treatment is the same: a few racy photographs, maybe a live meltdown. Now, instead of going to the nerve doctor, there's a publicist to call in the morning. We never stopped exhibiting these women; we just moved the show, from the hospitals to the grocery-store checkout line. If anything, it's easier than ever to attend. You had to pay a penny to visit Bedlam, but you can visit *Perez Hilton* for free.

We need public hysterics because the idea of the "madwoman" is intimately connected to our ideas of womanhood in general. Once we knew that some women had hysteria, all women had it, or at least 75 percent of them. Women who cry, women who laugh. Women who like sex, women who don't like sex. Drunk, old, poor, queer. Every woman has something wrong with her, if you go looking for it. And while mental illness and addiction violate every rule that a "nice" woman is supposed to live by—rendering her disobedient, abrasive, emotional, ugly—they confirm everything that misogynists suspect women to be at heart.

If all female sexuality is inappropriate, no one is more inappropriate than the woman who rips her clothes off or kisses strangers. If all female emotions are irrational, no one is more irrational than the woman utterly deprived of reason. If all women are weak and need to be protected and controlled by men, no one in the world is more obviously weak than the woman you have to lock up for her own safety. The madwoman is where the trainwreck gains velocity, becomes a phenomenon, not because other women fall short of her sins, but because we monitor women for those sins in order to prove that women are mad.

So, when we get a live one, we parade the evidence: make her a painting, or a photograph, or a live show, or the cover of *Star Magazine*. By breaking the rules of femininity, these women confirm that femininity is a necessary containment structure; that, if you took the chains off, women would run amok. But, to have a rule, we need rule-breakers. So we give you Courtney Love. We give you Amy Winehouse. We give you Amanda Bynes.

For men, the point of this is obvious: It keeps them distrustful of women, ready and eager to laugh at or dislike women, and quietly, constantly assured that they don't really have to take women all that seriously. Which, since most of the culture is aimed at conveying that message anyway, is not surprising. But in truth, men are not the primary beneficiary of all this rule-defining.

The degrading, degraded female images are really aimed

at you: Yes, you, the nice, normal girl trying to figure out how to behave in public. We give you a constant stream of images and a whole lot of very good reasons to play by the rules and never, ever let the act slip. Because you aren't a nice girl who spends one night a year playing dress-up as a monster. You're a monster who spends 364 nights a year playing dress-up as a nice girl.

•

Anatomy of a Trainwreck

VALERIE SOLANAS

"I ask you, ladies and gentlemen," the talk-show host asked, "have you ever heard anything more sick and perverted than this woman?"

This was 1967, on the set of the conservative *Alan Burke Show*. The woman in question had shown up, against her friends' advice, in answer to Burke's open call for lesbians willing to be interviewed on-air. She had, apparently, kept her cool throughout most of the show, while Burke taunted her with questions about her sexual experience with men: "What's the matter, Valerie, can't get one? Didn't anyone ever take you to prom?"

Valerie Solanas had been sexually abused from a young age. She had borne two children by the time she was fif-

teen, one of them quite possibly her father's. We don't know
if she told any of this to Alan Burke; the producers didn't
keep a tape of her appearance. Anything we know about
the episode comes from interviews that her friends gave to
biographers after the fact. One thing they are all clear on
is that, after enough of these questions, Valerie had begun
crying and cursing at Burke. The producers cut her mic, and
Burke walked off the set.

Valerie chased him across the stage and tried to hit him
with a chair.

The frightening thing about *The Alan Burke Show*, in retrospect, is that well before anyone knew who Valerie Solanas was—before she made any headlines, or did any of the
shocking things that would eventually make her a house-
hold name—it established her role in public life. From the
very first moment she showed up, on Burke's set and in the
living rooms of his viewers, she was a madwoman in a cage;
a scary, angry, man-hating lesbian that you could poke with
a stick until she lashed out.

By the end of the next year, of course, she would have a
résumé to fit the job description. Solanas's mental health is
not really in question: In an attempt to murder Andy Warhol, art critic Mario Amaya, and Warhol's manager Fred
Hughes, she shot Warhol in the gut and Amaya in the hip.
The gun jammed while she had it aimed it at Hughes's head.
After the shooting, she spent time in mental institutions,
public housing, or homeless. She was paranoid, occasionally

violent, and by the end of her life, she was a derelict, known to the local police as "Scab Lady" for her habit of self-mutilating by stabbing herself repeatedly with a fork.

But to say that she was crazy misses the point that she was also a philosopher of craziness. Flash back to La Salpêtrière, and the collection of women housed there: the addicts, the prostitutes, the homeless, the queer. All the women society no longer had a use for. From this cast-off and collected scum of the earth arose the whole idea of the "madwoman." And from a madwoman (a prostitute, a queer woman, a homeless woman, an eventual addict) arose *SCUM*.

The *SCUM Manifesto*—which Valerie was already self-publishing and giving lectures on before she met Warhol—was meant to build a utopia out of the women who had been thrown away, a perfect world run by "those females least embedded in the male 'Culture' . . . too uncivilized to give a shit for anyone's opinion of them, too arrogant to respect 'Daddy' or the wisdom of the Ancients, who trust only their own animal, gutter instincts." The world of ruined women, in her view, was the only world worth living in: "Unhampered by propriety, niceness, discretion, public opinion, 'morals,' the respect of assholes, always funky, always dirty, SCUM gets around."

It was less a refutation of misogyny than a script-flip. Women were emotional? Well, "having a crudely constructed nervous system that is easily upset by the least display of emotion or feeling, the male tries to ensure a 'social'

code that ensures perfect blandness, unsullied by the slightest trace of feeling or upsetting opinion." Women were led
astray by sexual appetites? Behold: The male was "obsessed
with screwing; he'll swim through a river of snot, wade
nostril-deep through a river of vomit, if he thinks there'll
be a friendly pussy awaiting him." It was an erudite satire,
calling on the whole history of women's mental health—
Solanas had done both her undergraduate and postgraduate work in psychology; the *Manifesto* takes time to flip off
Freud by declaring that men's personal deficiencies are due
to "pussy envy"—but written from the other side of the
mirror. A tour of La Salpêtrière, with Louise Augustine
holding the camera.

In another decade there might have been a place for her
to land, or at least a label by which she could be understood:
Feminism, queer theory, and punk have all claimed her
since. But in the early 1960s, Valerie's society of dirty, angry, fucked-up women didn't exist. She was writing to will
it into being. She tried to physically incarnate it, by writing
a play (the immortally titled *Up Your Ass*) wherein Bongi Perez—sort of a roughed-up, wisecracking, queer lady street
Jesus—heckles "nice," brainwashed women out of their il-
lusions. At one point, a man tells her that she's ugly, so she
pulls him behind the bushes and fucks him to prove a point;
in the grand finale, a frustrated suburban mother strangles
her whiny son to death so that she can go pick up chicks
with Bongi. It's that kind of play.

It would have been Valerie's world, on stage. Made real, and corporeal, and with her at its center. In the story of her life, nothing was so important, not even the *SCUM Manifesto*. (She'd thrown that to publisher Maurice Girodias in an attempt to get out of a bad contract; he'd wanted a novel, and refused to publish what she gave him—until she was in the news). It was the play that she wanted Andy Warhol to film, that she gave to him, that he tried to make disappear by offering her a movie role instead; it was the play that, finally, Warhol claimed he'd just plain lost, and refused to return to her.

How could he have known what she would do? How could a woman who had already taken so much humiliation—sexual abuse, poverty, losing her children; homelessness, begging, sex with men she hated, to stay on the right side of starvation; being laughed at and booed by a studio audience; a night when Warhol incited a friend to call Valerie a "disgusting dyke" and then sneered when she said she'd been molested—be expected to do anything but take one more insult, a very minor insult, a lost copy, as par for the course?

How could anyone know what Valerie would do, when a powerful man tried to make her work disappear?

But she did it. It was the culmination of her suspicions—ever since the *Alan Burke Show*—that she was being set up, that someone didn't want her to be heard, someone was trying to turn her into a joke. It was the Mob, and Warhol and

Girodias both worked for it, and they'd taken her uterus and replaced it with a radio transmitter so they could track her everywhere. And, after she did it, she never published another book. She fell into the world of the Mob, the world where Valerie was only Scab Lady, and there fell silent.

But Girodias published the *Manifesto*; it was Girodias who told the world that SCUM was an acronym for "Society for Cutting Up Men," and called her genocidal in his preface. Lucky her, she even became a valid talking point outside the art world. Feminism had been on the rise, and now conservatives could point to its logical outcome: some man-hating, crazy lesbian who wanted to kill all men. You couldn't say that there were none. One of them made the news. And you couldn't, in good conscience, recommend that any nice girl get mixed up with the criminal element. The fame lasted, although, thanks to Girodias's contract, Valerie never saw a dime: As late as 1977, *The Village Voice* would call her up and run interviews of her ranting about the Mob.

Valerie Solanas meant to stand for the dirty, angry, fucked-up, thrown-away women of the world. And she did: not as messiah, but as bogeyman. When she was just a writer, no one wanted her. But she was more than marketable as a criminal, and a cautionary tale. Ladies and gentlemen, have you ever heard anything more sick and perverse than this woman?

There is one piece of Solanas's writing that, unaccountably, never made it to publication. No one has ever published that play. But copies of it can be found online, if you dig for them. Each page is stamped, "From the Collection of THE ANDY WARHOL MUSEUM."

•

From most vantage points, Valerie Solanas is indefensible. She wasn't upset or misunderstood or under stress: She was actually crazy. And, though most people fear the mentally ill unless we can pity them, Valerie's illness never rendered her a passive victim. She was continually cruel, even flat-out abusive, to the people in her life—not just the snooty Factory denizens, but people who were genuinely kind to her, including the feminists who organized to help her during her trial. Her sexual politics were not so perfect that she was beyond criticism; radical as Valerie was, her thoughts on transgender women (something she elaborates on quite a bit in *Up Your Ass*) could be corrosively ugly and even bigoted. And, oh, yeah, *she tried to murder three people*. What line of defense can you concoct for that?

Maybe this one: As art critic Catherine Lord points out, eight years before anyone knew the name "Valerie Solanas," Norman Mailer stabbed his wife to settle an argument at a party. Two years before that, William S. Burroughs got drunk and accidentally shot his wife in the head while attempting to demonstrate his marksmanship. And yet, in your lifetime, you are strikingly unlikely to ever meet someone who informs you that the notorious murderer, William S. Burroughs, also wrote books. Norman Mailer served time in Bellevue, but somehow, an explanation of his life story tends to open with "author" rather than "lunatic."

Or you could go back to Kurt Cobain. Poor Kurt, dead Kurt, Kurt who suffered: He was a heroin addict, he was deeply and intentionally difficult, he called up at least one journalist and threatened to kill her, he had his daughter taken away when she was two weeks old, and (oh, yeah) he shot himself. And, in all of this, the take-away for his tween fanbase was that his wife was crazy.

Mental illness and addiction ruin women—make them sideshows, dirty jokes, bogeymen, objects of moral panic—but they seem to add to a man's mystique. No one made fun of Kurt's track marks; they built him a cult. Just as, throughout history, men have built cults around the sacred, illuminating madness of Antonin Artaud, or Vaslav Nijinsky, or David Foster Wallace, or Jack Kerouac, or Iggy Pop, or Jackson Pollock, or Vincent Van Gogh. That list, taken in a different light, reads Schizophrenic, Schizophrenic, Suicide, Drunk, Got So High He Can't Remember the 1970s, Drunk, and Suicide. (Comma, Plus That Thing with the Ear.) Yet the diagnoses don't end them, or even really define them. Instead, their struggles elevate them, make them special: We all understand that genius and madness are connected. At least, we do when the genius is male.

Lou Reed was a brilliant, queer kid who reportedly had a psychotic break, moved to New York City, befriended Warhol, and became a legend. Valerie Solanas was a brilliant, queer kid who had a psychotic break, moved to New York City, befriended Warhol, and had her play thrown away and got called a "disgusting dyke" at parties. Lou hated Valerie to the very end of his days (sample lyric: "There's something wrong if she's alive right now") and I will always love Lou. But I hope that, from his throne in Curmudgeonly Rock Dude Heaven, even Lou can see that the difference between what happened to him and what happened to Valerie was pretty much Valerie's entire point.

The world is the world. Masculinity is supposed to be brave, risk-taking, rebellious; femininity is supposed to be sweet, agreeable, people-pleasing. Madness makes the one gender riskier and braver; it makes the other less compliant and harder to deal with. And so it is that a male painter can get wasted and drive his car into a tree to impress his mistress (a mistress who is, I need to stress, in the car at the time) and only add to the legend that is Jackson Pollock, whereas if a former child actress gets drunk and passes out in her SUV, innocence itself has died.

But what does this do to the girl in the car? What does it do to any woman who is sick, or fragile, or dealing with actual, no-fooling mental illness or addiction?

The standard excuse for trainwreck-shaming is that people want "role models"—that celebrities have influence, that they shape young minds, that they must behave correctly lest people imitate them, and so on and so forth. But our standard way of treating "bad role models" is almost exactly calculated to harm those young minds that most need care. If your daughter starts binge drinking, or crying in public, or passing out at events, you don't chase her around the yard with a garden rake, calling her a disgusting whore. And if you do, her sister is not going to come to you the next time she has a problem.

Shame is not a sufficient treatment for mental illnesses, or for addiction. In fact, there's evidence that it makes certain illnesses worse: In one study, recovering alcoholics with greater tendencies toward shame (that is, an overwhelming sense that they were bad human beings; this is opposed to guilt, a reasonable belief that you've done something wrong) were actually more likely to relapse, and they drank more when relapsing than people with lower shame levels. Mental illness is not helped, or even effectively and accurately portrayed, by broadcasting theatrical, compromising, shocking images of mentally ill people. The only cause aided by that is the very old, Bedlam-circa-1700s cause of dehumanizing the ill: turning them into monsters, and Others, creatures to be feared and laughed at instead of people to be loved and helped.

So, no: We are not helping Lindsay Lohan or Amanda Bynes by treating them like circus freaks. Nor are we helping any of the many women with similar struggles—

women who need therapy or medication, or women who need to get sober, or women who are simply at the ends of their ropes and don't see an option other than imploding or lashing out.

Not only is shame not helpful in treating mental illness or addiction, it also fails to justify its apparent *raison d'être* in the trainwreck narrative. It doesn't help instill "good values"; instead, it creates a world in which women are afraid of themselves—where every girl lives like the lead in a werewolf movie, constantly monitoring herself for signs that she's turning into a wild animal. Women with serious illnesses are being taught to hate themselves by the ongoing public display of madwomen, but so are women who are merely unhappy, or having a bad day. Female emotion itself is being portrayed as a destructive force that must be tamped down, contained, and (if at all possible) totally denied, because if it ever breaks through and becomes visible, that woman will become dirty, shameful, and disgusting.

I don't know of a single person, male or female, who has ever solved their problems by refusing to admit that they had problems. But that kind of denial is what we teach women, every day of their lives, by telling them that their unhappiness is not only inconvenient, but flat-out pathological. Exhibiting madwomen creates a world where any woman can be called "crazy," and dismissed, if she says something you don't want to hear. It creates a climate where women are constantly inspected for signs of out-of-control

emotionalism or sexual mania. But, worse than this, it creates a world where women who are suffering are afraid to
ask for the help they need to save their own lives—a world
where the only alternative to being made a spectacle or a
trainwreck is to disappear.

4

DEATH

In February 2012, I had a party to attend. It was an ordinary affair, in one of the many hundreds of semi-respectable and totally forgettable bars down at the lower end of Manhattan—the kind of place that has both fanciful martini toppings and a jukebox in the corner. I mention this because the only thing I remember about the party is that jukebox. Every hour or half-hour, one patron's playlist would end and another one would begin. And so it would start up once again, the same song everyone else had picked, its enormous climax blaring through the bar noise: *And IIIIIIII will always love youuuuuuu.*

Whitney Houston had died that afternoon. The song was their way of remembering her. But, after a few repetitions and a few drinks, it began to seem less like public mourning and more like a cruel joke.

There had been a time, certainly, when we loved Whitney. When I was a little girl, Whitney was a princess. We learned her songs in choir. (To this day, I can't hear the line "You can't take away my *dig*-ni-*ty*" without imagining it in the voice of two dozen fumbling second-graders who weren't entirely sure what that last word meant.) She was a child's perfect embodiment of glamour, a beautiful lady who appeared on late-night TV in sparkling gowns, a romantic heroine—this very song came from a movie my best friend and I had stolen from her mother and watched in secret, because (we had been led to believe) it was one of the most beautiful love stories ever told, and also too dirty for us to watch—and an idol. I had been in a car with an adult woman, my friend's mother, who made us shut up for the entirety of "I Will Always Love You" when it came on the radio, and who had actual tears on her face when it was over. We loved Whitney. The little girls and the mothers, together. In the days when we loved her, it seemed impossible that we could stop.

We stopped. Suddenly, brutally, totally. By 2002, Whitney was a ghost: Frail, abused, addicted, her enormous voice hollowed out, whispering her way through an interview with Diane Sawyer where a discussion of whether Bobby Brown hit her was derailed by the fact that Bobby had stepped into the room to watch her talk. (Brown: "No, no, no. I would never." Houston: "What does 'hitting' mean?") Headlines flashed onto the screen: WHITNEY DYING. WHITNEY IS A WALKING SKELETON. MYSTERIOUS INJURY MAY LEAVE WHITNEY SCARRED. WHITNEY DENIES THAT SHE'S DEAD.

The interview became a joke (she said "Crack is whack!"

She sassed Sawyer!) and the jokes became GIFs and memes, and the GIFs and memes became who she was: As late as 2009, *Buzzfeed* was repackaging clips from it under the title "The 10 Best Moments From Whitney Houston's Infamous Diane Sawyer Interview." ("This interview . . . [from] when Whitney was still all drugged up is the best Whitney interview ever. Relive the magic with these 10 clips.") We got more clips; got a reality show, *Being Bobby Brown*, filmed while Brown was on trial for domestic abuse; got, finally, footage of Whitney admitting to the drugs, fighting with Bobby, screaming "Kiss my ass" (it played on repeat on *The Soup*) and telling the camera that sometimes she got constipated enough that Brown had to pull feces out of her with his hand.

We took away your dig-ni-ty, Whitney. It turned out that we could, and that we wanted to. We did it for fun, because it was funny, because it made a good *BuzzFeed* list. We did it because she was a black addict, using a drug associated with poor black addicts. We did it because it was just what everyone else was doing.

Then she fell face-down in a bathtub. And she drowned there. Details about precisely which parts of her face had been hemorrhaging, and which chemicals were in her system, were already on their way to us thanks to whichever proud journalists were working the celebrity death beat that evening. The *National Enquirer* would find their way into the funeral and put a photo of her lying in the casket on its front page. (Whitney, this time, had not denied that she was dead. But, being notoriously responsible journalists, they still went looking for proof.) The Diane Sawyer interview was being repackaged, re-aired, re-posted; what had provided "The Best" moments before her death would provide *Mediaite*, two days after her death, with "The Most Disturbing Moment." And tonight her song was playing, promising eternal devotion, the kind of love that never turns on its object, never mocks her, never views her pain coldly, never fades with time. *Always love, always love, **always** love.* She sang it over and over, a torn fragment of Whitney's princess past echoing through the air and under every conversation we had.

Because now, now that our idol had fallen bleeding into the cold water and died there, we were ready to love Whitney Houston again. We were ready to tell ourselves that we always had. We weren't forgiving Whitney Houston, that night. We were forgiving ourselves. And the more I heard her, the less certain I was that our forgiveness had been earned.

This is where it's all headed. What the whole trainwreck industry is pushing for: the one form of permanent redemption that the culture freely allows to a woman who is mad, bad, and dangerous to know. After all the flame-outs, the breakdowns, jokes, the failures, the surveillance, the invasions, the dehumanization—after all the years of hating these women, and punishing them—the one happy ending that we as a culture will accept is the moment where it all falls in on her. And we all get to gather around the coffin, and sigh, and say that it's a shame.

We love our dead girls. We love them pretty, and we love them young: Aside from Houston, who was a practically ancient 48 years old at the time of her death, we have Amy Winehouse (27), Anna Nicole Smith (39), Princess Diana (36), Janis Joplin (27), Marilyn Monroe (36), Jayne Mansfield (34), Judy Garland (47), Zelda Fitzgerald (47) . . . and on and on, further and further back in time, probably back to the first woman who ever picked up a drink she couldn't put down.

The outpouring of love and grief that these women receive, in the wake of their deaths, tends to wipe their records clean. Amy Winehouse's death caused much of the press to turn a complete 180 on her: *NME Magazine*, which had nominated her as one of its "Villains of the Year" in 2008, promptly rounded up celebrity quotes on her greatness once she was dead and thus incapable of further villainy. We've covered the most infamous profile of Winehouse, in which a reporter went to her house at four in the morning to cover the "little scabs that raid her face" and a photo of "Winehouse's blurry face, taken from above with a phone in one hand and a gigantic penis in her mouth." But it's also notable that *Rolling Stone*, the same publication that made

this story the cover, published tribute upon tribute after
her death, opening one rapturous article by lamenting the
fact that her "remarkable musical achievements were often
overshadowed by her tumultuous personal life." Well, yeah:
You're the ones who told the world about the dick-suck-
ing photo. Where did you *think* the attention was going to
gravitate?

Similarly, during the massive international spectacle
of Princess Diana's death and funeral—the televised me-
morial service, with 3 million people in attendance and
2.5 billion watching at home; the streets full of flowers
and weeping citizenry; the Elton John rewrite of "Candle
in the Wind," which became the best-selling single of all
time—it was hard to even remember that the girl who was
currently being eulogized as England's Rose (*You belong to
heaven! Our nation lost without your soul!*) had, in the last decade or so of her life, been portrayed as "crazy," bulimic,
and self-harming, addicted to media attention, and the subject of stories about how she'd thrown herself down flights
of stairs and driven through Paris wearing only a fur coat
and underpants.

It did linger, a bit: It was too entrenched in her persona
to do otherwise. In 1999, *The New York Times* endorsed
author Sally Bedel Smith's posthumous diagnosis of
"borderline personality disorder," and called Diana "un-
predictable, egocentric, aggressive, insecure, manipulative,
paranoid, possessive, easily bored, uneducated and a habit-

ual liar." (Sub-headline: "The author's diagnosis explains why Diana was so rotten, but not why others seemed to like her.") And yet, in the sea of flowers and tears and piano ballads, all seemed forgotten. Alive, she was a madwoman and a blight on the British crown. Dead, she was Ophelia, lost and lovely, garlanded and mourned as she passed downstream.

In addition to all the public and private hypocrisies and the revisions of history, there is an even seamier side of the Cult of the Dead Wreck to address. There is (sorry about this, folks) the necrophilia.

Marilyn Monroe was also hated when she died. Her *Some Like It Hot* costar Tony Curtis said that filming a love scene with her was like "kissing Hitler"; Billy Wilder, who'd been her director on *The Seven-Year Itch* and *Hot*, refused to invite her to the premiere of the second picture because of her chronic lateness and erratic behavior, and once publicly claimed, "I'm the only director who ever made two pictures with Monroe. It behooves the Screen Directors Guild to award me a Purple Heart." Arthur Miller, her husband at the time, told Wilder that Monroe had been pregnant while shooting, had needed half-days, and had miscarried. Wilder replied that the story was too big for him *not* to talk trash: "I have been besieged by newspapermen from as far as London, Paris and Berlin for a statement," he said. "The conclusions reached by the columnist from his own research would have been twice as vicious had I not submitted to the interview." A *Ladies' Home Journal* profile of her was killed for being too sympathetic. Monroe was aware of all this, and she was angry about it: "An actor is supposed to be a sensitive instrument," she said in her last interview. "Isaac Stern takes good care of his violin. What if everybody jumped on his violin?"

And then, before the interview was even printed, she died. The hate, predictably, went away. What came in its place was infinitely creepier: Her death became a fetish.

MARILYN MONROE KILLS SELF, ran a full-page headline in the *New York Mirror*. The first detail included in the sub-headline was "Found nude in bed." The woman who'd spent the last years of her life railing at the idea that she was just a dumb, pretty blonde, just a joke, had the spectacle of her naked, helpless body trotted out in just about every outlet that covered her passing.

The circumstances of her death, too, have attracted a fetishist's possessive attention. Aside from the conspiracy theories (*Murdered by Kennedys! Driven mad by the CIA!*) showbiz-memorabilia collector Todd Mueller raved to *Vanity Fair* in 2008 about a cache of "amazing stuff" that was about to enter the Monroe market, "including the half-drunk bottle of champagne she used to wash the pills down that night." The Wikipedia article for "Death of Marilyn Monroe" (she and Princess Diana are among the few celebrities to have a whole article specifically dedicated to the circumstances of their demise) shows an alarming specificity in reporting that Monroe was buried in "the 'Cadillac of caskets'—a hermetically sealed antique-silver-finished 48-ounce (heavy gauge) solid bronze 'masterpiece' casket lined with champagne-colored satin-silk." Photos of Monroe in that casket circulate online, and show up in any Google search related to her death. So do photos of her on the autopsy table.

Finally, Hugh Hefner, the man who'd leaked Monroe's nudes in the first issue of *Playboy* decades before the phrase "leaking nudes" was even in the lexicon—he became an instant celebrity; she had to apologize for the photos, and feared for her career—bought the crypt next to Monroe's for $75,000. It was a gruesome joke, "sleeping with" the woman he'd almost ruined, and doing so without her consent—claiming her in death, as he'd claimed the right to exploit her in life. "I'm a sucker for blondes and she is the ultimate blonde," Hefner told *CBS Los Angeles*. "It has a completion notion to it. I will be spending the rest of my eternity with Marilyn."

Meanwhile, the vault above Monroe's went to Richard Poncher, a man who reportedly told his wife, "If I croak, if you don't put me upside down over Marilyn, I'll haunt you the rest of my life." She made sure he was flipped over in the coffin to accommodate his wishes. Or, at least, to accommodate them until 2009, when the good widow Poncher put his spot up for auction on eBay. Bidding started at $500,000.

With the difficult woman inside removed, Monroe's body—that much-remarked-upon, much-commodified object—was once again the property of the public. She belonged to us. We had the right to know. To see. To lie next to; to lie on top of. Who was to stop us?

And then, there is Lana Del Rey: The Dead Girl Come Alive. The girl who was, as her first album title informed us, *born* to die. Her entire career to date has been about compressing the trainwreck into a performance, a marketable archetype: lovely, "crazy," drawn to the wrong men, and doomed to die young. In song after song—"Off to the Races" is a prime offender, but then, so is most of her first album—her voice ascends into a breathy, cooing, little-girl register ("Hi . . . who, *me*?") that mimics Marilyn Monroe's. (A register that, by the way, was not Monroe's real voice, either—in audio tapes of interviews, she's full-throated and assertive, and she descends by about half an octave. She *was* an actress, after all.) In the video for "National Anthem," Del Rey actually plays Monroe, and in "Body Electric" she's haunted by her ghost. In others she flips through tabloids that describe her own out-of-control downward spiral; she holds a gun to her head; she is a naked, bloodied corpse dragged from a Diana-esque car wreck; she's drowned by her lover in a swimming pool. She writes songs about loving it when her man hits her, about getting mixed up with a man who loves guns and heroin, about loving a man who "likes his girls insane." About her own death ("When I get to heaven, please let me bring my man") and sometimes her own suicide: ("I wish I was deeeeead," cue Marilyn voice, *"dead like you"*).

She's said that elsewhere. In one infamous interview she told *The Guardian*, "I wish I was dead already." She might not have meant it literally—most of Del Rey's songs are predicated on sounding as if she died several decades ago—but it resonated, in part because it was the one line that seemed to sum up the entire Del Rey brand.

After all, she is right about one thing: Death is more glamorous than living in the wreck. After Winehouse's death, for example, news outlets and social media were filled with thoughts about the tragedy of addiction, and Winehouse's helplessness in the face of it. It's substantially harder to find anyone expressing similar sentiments about the still-alive Courtney Love. And everyone remembers Monroe. They may also remember that she had a "rival," the similarly blonde and curvy Jayne Mansfield, who was supposedly decapitated in a car wreck. (She wasn't, but people liked the story.) Yet you'd be hard-pressed to find anyone who could name the third member of the so-called "Three M's": Mamie Van Doren, who is alive and well and posing for topless photos as an octogenarian in California.

But there is something else in play here, some older

narrative. It's instructive to look to the music itself—to the genre and style that Del Rey, like Amy Winehouse before her, chose to signify an appetite for self-destruction. "I'm a big jazz aficionado," Del Rey told *Fader* in 2014. "Hopefully my next foray will be into jazz." Or you could look to the name she moans, on "Blackest Day," to epitomize her appetite for self-destruction: *All I hear is Billie Holiday. It's all I play.*

She's right about that, too. On some level, Lana Del Rey—like Whitney Houston, like Amy Winehouse, like any number of women—is just playing Billie.

•

Anatomy of a Trainwreck

BILLIE HOLIDAY

"I was playing a gig in New Jersey, walking across the yard, and I heard it over a loudspeaker," said pianist Carl Drinkard. "'Jazz singer Billie Holiday was arrested in her hospital room for possession of narcotics.' I looked at Be-Bop Sam, a little trumpet player, and I said, 'Lady's gonna die.' I knew it just like I knew my name."

Drinkard was right. Billie Holiday—Lady Day, to anyone who knew her; Eleanora Fagan, at birth—was dying. She was an alcoholic, up to a bottle of gin a day, in the hospital because her liver was failing. When a bag of heroin was confiscated from her room, she was arrested and quickly began going through withdrawal. Possibly, she could have survived the cirrhosis. Possibly, she could have survived the heroin withdrawal. But she could not do both. Her body couldn't handle two crises at the same time.

Drinkard was not the only one planning around Lady Day's death that day. Her ghostwriter, William Dufty, was trying to sell an article to *Confidential*, so that he could get her money to keep the heroin coming. *Playboy* and *Esquire* had already turned him down—Billie Holiday had been done to death; the topic had been exhausted—and *Confidential* would only give him a shot if he found some new angle.

"And I said to myself, new angle, new angle, new angle, and I was desperate, so I said, what about 'Heroin Saved My Life,'" Dufty told Holiday archivist Linda Kuehl, "and he said terrific. They were concerned with one thing, that they get it in the magazine while she was still alive, and I couldn't guarantee that she would live."

She did live long enough to get the money, but not to spend it. The wad of fifty-dollar bills from *Confidential* was on her when she died, and it would turn out to be the only money she had in the world.

Billie Holiday, the most celebrated singer of her generation—hell, of *any* generation—had spent most of her adult life flat broke. For one thing, she'd been convicted of heroin possession in 1947, and people with prison convictions could not play New York nightclubs that served alcohol. She was a New York jazz singer, and jazz singers made their living by playing nightclubs. "I could play in theaters and sing to an audience of kids who couldn't get in any bar. I could appear on radio or TV. I could appear in concerts at Town Hall or Carnegie Hall," she said. "That was OK. But if I opened my mouth in the crummiest bar in town, I was violating the law."

Record sales didn't help, either. She had been singing since the 1920s, and recording since 1935, but until 1944, when she signed with Decca, she didn't receive a cent in royalties. She performed for a flat fee. People could be tremendous Billie Holiday fans without ever once paying Billie Holiday to sing. Articles "by" Billie Holiday, on the topic of her addiction—"I'm Cured for Good"; "Billie's Tragic Life"; "Can a Dope Addict Come Back"; etc.—were how she tried to make up for the income her actual addiction cut off.

If this is starting to sound familiar, it should. Billie Holiday was working the image-rehabilitation circuit, no different than Whitney doing Diane Sawyer. She wrote a memoir with Dufty, *Lady Sings the Blues*, that told the world she was sober and in a great relationship. (She was neither.) She recorded a "comeback" album with a more commercial pop sound—*Lady in Satin*, and in this particular year, "commercial pop" meant a full orchestra rather than a jazz band—

that was marketed as being based on her tragic life story. She even submitted to a Very Special Episode of television about her downfall and redemption, *The Comeback Story*, on ABC. She did everything we do now, but she did it for the first time.

Billie Holiday was born in 1915, at the very dawn of the modern era. Slavery had ended just fifty years prior; plenty of white people in the United States could still remember it, or had owned slaves themselves. And plenty of black Americans had actually survived being enslaved, even if they were children at the time. To give you an idea, the end of slavery was about as far removed from Billie Holiday's birth as Beatlemania is from you today: If you're under thirty-five, you might find it quaint, but your mother or grandmother probably remembers that first *Ed Sullivan Show* appearance like it happened yesterday.

And, as far as racial progress was concerned, it might as well have *been* yesterday. Racism still held an iron grip on the American consciousness and government. The world was still spectacularly cruel to young black girls. But Billie had to deal with all this, while also being one of the first entertainers to deal with the contemporary mechanisms of entertainment and celebrity, which came roaring and shuddering to life over the course of her career. Billie was, among other things, a test case: one of the first women in America who was prevented from selling her gift, and forced to sell her pain.

In some sense, it had always been part of her appeal. As biographer John Szwed notes, of the three songs most associated with Billie Holiday in her lifetime, all were about violence, and two were about death. "My Man," domestic abuse. "Gloomy Sunday," suicide. "Strange Fruit," a song about lynching that can suck the breath out of you to this day. It wasn't as if she didn't record light, sentimental love songs; there were dozens of them. But something about Billie made you remember the sad songs first: That weird, bruised voice, getting more worn and clawed-open every year, twisting its way through the songs. She always seemed to sing from the other side of something. As if pain were an ocean, a wide dark place she'd traveled; as if it were a country, and she had crossed the border and started sending reports back home.

And, yes, some part of that pain came from her life. From being born poor, to a mother who was young and unmarried, and never allowed to forget it. From giving herself an abortion as a teenager to avoid the life her mother had. From surviving an attempted rape by a neighbor—for which she and her mother were punished when they reported it.

"I'll never forget that night," she would later say, in *Lady Sings the Blues.* "It's the worst thing that can happen to a woman. And here it was happening to me when I was ten."

Her attacker led her into a brothel, claiming he was taking her there to meet her mother, and assaulted her after she fell asleep. Afterward, when Billie's mother took her to the police station in Baltimore, the law came crashing down on them both.

"[Instead] of treating me and Mom like somebody who went to the cops for help, they treated me like I'd killed somebody. They wouldn't let my mother take me home," she said. "I guess they had me figured for having enticed this old goat into the whorehouse or something. All I know for sure is they threw me into a cell."

Billie was deemed not to have sufficient adult supervision, torn away from her mother, and placed in an institution for wayward girls.

Later, there were her men, all of whom beat her. (One of them went at her with a whip for waking him up at night; one of them used to kick her in the ribs and stomach before she performed, telling her bandmates he had to "beat the shit out of her so she sings good.") There was the fact that she was a bisexual woman, in an age when most people didn't even know the word "bisexual"; there were the white women who adopted her as a part of their rebellious phase and dropped her when it suited them. There was racism: national tours where she couldn't reliably eat in restaurants or use public bathrooms, and shows where she was forced to wear blackface on stage because she looked pale under the lights, and club owners couldn't risk the scandal that might ensue if she were mistaken for a white woman performing with black men.

And then, at last, there was heroin. Which seems, in retrospect, less like a downfall than a logical outcome: Who could be surprised that a woman who'd experienced almost every variety of human pain found herself drawn to the world's strongest anaesthetic? But still, it was the pain that Billie had to spend her life justifying, explaining, publicly defending, and, ultimately, just plain selling to an increasingly white, middle-class audience who were eager for a look at the much-mythologized underworld figure—the criminal, drug-addicted black jazz musician— and who drank up her music for a taste of how the other half lived.

"Everybody was happy about the crowds that used to flock to the theater. People were standing when the place opened in the morning. People were still standing for the last show at night. Everybody thought this was great, except me," she said. "I thought people were just coming to see how high I was. 'They hope I'll fall on my face or something,' I used to say."

It was cruel treatment, especially for an artist of her caliber. Because Billie was not just good; she was not just great. She almost single-handedly created an art form. Before Billie, there were singers, and there were jazz musicians. Billie legitimized the idea of the jazz singer as a great musician in her own right: not someone propped up in front of the band, but a living, breathing, improvising part of it, someone whose recomposition and reinterpretations of the melody were as essential as any horn solo. No matter how sick she got, or how hard it was to sing, when she sang, genius happened. And it never happened the same way twice.

Critics are still figuring out exactly how she worked. Some of the things she did with tempo had no antecedent in Western music, outside a few experimental pieces by Chopin. Biographer Donald Clarke says that only Louis Armstrong was a predecessor, and only Ella Fitzgerald was a peer. Other than that, every jazz singer whose name we know—Sarah Vaughan, Nina Simone, Chet Baker, Frank Sinatra—came after Billie, and was directly influenced by her. More than that, the archetype she created in the public consciousness, the tormented female singer who exorcised her demons on stage—because she was adamant that she actually *felt* everything she sang, every time; "When I sing, it affects me so much I get sick. It takes all the strength out of me," she said—is found in every corner of music. She's responsible for everyone from Erykah Badu and Lauryn Hill to Tori Amos and Fiona Apple, from Amy and Lana to Joni and Janis.

Still, when Billie gave her historic Carnegie Hall concert in 1956—the moment some historians point to as the official canonization of jazz, the moment when it stopped being low entertainment and became high American art—she had to do it under the guise of tragedy and comeback, with a white man standing next to her and reading excerpts from *Lady Sings the Blues* so that the audience could appreciate how her appeal sprang from her hard-knock life.

And the knocks got harder. The public-rehabilitation circuit was not kind to Billie. *Lady in Satin* was dismissed: It wasn't "real jazz." She started to get too sick to make it through the sessions, too nervous to get through them without drinking more and more. Her voice hollowed out to a rasp. As for the book, well: Though Billie's pain was fine to look at, hearing about it was another thing: Did she have to sound so *angry*?

"There is so much of human suffering, sensitivity and music in her voice," wrote Harry Lieb, an attorney who worked on the book. "The book, therefore comes as a disappointment, as if in her autobiography she had written to put herself in the worst possible light." He called it "a series of gripes, with a few scandal items," and noted that "the cuss words get very tiresome when they are repeated over and over again."

Lieb believed that Billie's story should "evoke sympathy, pity, and understanding," but he apparently had trouble sympathizing with the woman herself. She failed to provide him with the tragedy he was looking for. Reviewers were no kinder: J. Saunders Redding, of the *Baltimore Afro-American*, sniffed at Holiday's "tragically disordered background," and, once again, called her out for cussing: "This

reviewer is no squeamish prude, but Billie Holiday and William Dufty use language so raw with so little warrant that there were times when this reviewer got 'real sick.'"
And these were the reactions she'd gotten from people who believed she'd even *worked* on the book—plenty of people believed her white ghostwriter had concocted it wholesale, rather than working from interviews and dictation—or who believed the story therein. Which plenty of people did not. The attempted rape was singled out as particularly unbelievable. Her biographers had to prove it, several times over, before it entered the official story of Billie Holiday's life.

"My book is just a bitch," Billie wrote to Dufty. "Did you see that shit that man from my birthplace Baltimore wrote? He even said my Mom and Dad were stinkers for having me. I am sick of the whole goddamn thing. You tell people the truth and you stink."

And so, she limped on. Getting sicker, getting more infamous. Letting the rumors fly and the people stare, having to prove herself all over again every time she opened her mouth: "I'm not supposed to get a toothache, I'm not supposed to get nervous; I can't throw up or get sick to my stomach; I'm not supposed to get the flu or have a sore throat," she said. "I'm supposed to go out there and look pretty and sing good and smile and I'd just better. Why? Because I'm Billie Holiday and I've been in trouble."

And she stayed in trouble, until she was in that hospital

bed, under police guard, and by that point so famously sick that she got to read the early write-ups of her own death in the paper. BILLIE HOLIDAY IS DYING OF DOPE AND ALCOHOL ADDICTION, read one headline. BILLIE DOOMED, ran another.

"We're all doomed, baby," she told the nurse. "What the hell else is news?"

And then she was gone, at forty-four-years-old, giving a suitably tragic ending to the world that had loved her pain.

•

Death seals the deal, for trainwrecks. It grants them their glamour. It makes them, not worthy of attention—they always have that; it's our primary weapon against them—but worthy of love. And that love, I would submit, is half nostalgia and half relief. It's the care we give, once we're not being asked to care any more.

For all our fetishization of celebrity death, the fact is, we can usually see it coming from miles away. When Billie Holiday got mixed up with heroin in the 1930s, it might have been a mistake, something she got into without knowing she couldn't get back out. But, in the twenty-first century, no one is under the impression that a crack or heroin addict is destined to live a long, healthy life. Everyone has heard the AA definition of alcoholism—"progressive, incurable, and fatal"—often enough to know that a history of DUIs or public intoxication doesn't speak well for that person's health. And everyone understands that mental illnesses like bipolar disorder or schizophrenia, or even severe cases of depression, can and do kill people.

We understand all of this, that is, until it comes to female celebrities. For them, we persist in enjoying the spectacle: turning Anna Nicole Smith's dazed, drug-addled public incoherence, or Whitney's unconvincing denials, or even Amy Winehouse's progressive and frightening emaciation, into our own campy entertainment, sarcastically branding it "magical" until the day of the overdose, when it finally stops being funny.

We typically reserve the death penalty for people who have committed extremely serious offenses. If these women have to pass away before we can forgive them, or even like them, it would stand to reason that they'd done something wrong. Yet, in almost every case, they were their own worst victims. To starve in public, or to stay in an abusive relationship, or to need alcohol or prescription drugs or street drugs to make it through the day, is a statement of pain, not of hostility. They terrorized us by being themselves.

Which makes death an extremely satisfying solution. These women, the trainwrecks, have offended us by being *unfeminine*, by being other than what a "good" woman should be. In Whitney's case, or Billie's, by being black women making good in a white man's world. In Marilyn's, by being overtly sexual in the buttoned-up 1950s. In Amy Winehouse's case, by being a girl with the hard-living, brawling lifestyle and foul mouth of a tough guy. They have offended us by succeeding despite the countless social structures and conventions that try to prevent women like them from even *existing*: by being wealthy, famous, public, without even bothering to obey the rules of quiet acquiescence that we try to drum into little girls' heads from the day they're born.

But death neutralizes them. It removes them from the public eye, definitively and permanently. And it shows, at last, that they really shouldn't have been who they were: shouldn't have taken those risks, done those things, said those words, lived that life. By dying, a trainwreck finally gives us the one statement we wanted to hear from her: that women like her really can't make it, and shouldn't be encouraged to try. That she really wasn't normal. That she didn't belong in our world.

A live trainwreck is an affront. A dead one is confirmation: No one can be that beautiful, that sexual, that successful, that free. Something has to go wrong; she has to pay, with her life, for breaking the rules. Breaking these women to the point of public emotional or mental collapse doesn't do enough to keep women scared of being like them, or of free and equal participation in the public sphere. We really do need a few heads to roll, to make sure that the message is clear. It's an ugly message, and a frightening one. Which is why it makes sense that we deny it, and wrap it up in sentiment; we cloak the harshest, and least permissible, expression of misogyny with the name of forgiveness, and of love.

Back to Princess Diana, and the world's most widely attended funeral. Underneath all the flowers and tears and pop songs, something infinitely darker was occurring: In the four weeks directly after her death, suicide rates among British women in Diana's age group rose by 45 percent. The same thing happened after Marilyn, and her eroticized death: The overall U.S. suicide rate rose by 12 percent. Monroe's case is typically explained as "suicide contagion," the fact that suicidal people have a greater tendency to act when a suicide is in the news. But Diana did not kill herself. She simply died, and so did women like her, by their own hand.

Put forth death as the ideal condition for troubled women—as something that makes them beautiful, forgivable, important—and plenty of troubled women will die. Not because these women are more gullible or foolish than anyone else, but because, in sufficiently dire straits (at the bottom of addiction, or depression, or simple loneliness) death already looks like an easier and better solution than continued pain and helplessness. Suicide-prevention experts know this. It's why they plead with journalists, over and over, not to make death look more appealing or glamorous than recovery.

Sober people understand that addicts and alcoholics are probably dying, but so do many addicts and alcoholics themselves; either the illness has them so tightly that they can't believe recovery is possible, or their lives (like Billie's life) are already so painful that death is no longer as frightening as it would be to a happy person. Neurotypical people understand that depression or mental illness result in suicide, but so do people with mental illness. The question is whether, knowing this, they still decide to take the medicine and make it through the day.

For those people, life is always the harder sell. Most therapies are focused on selling it, and even in the best of conditions, the best therapies can fail. They are infinitely more likely to do so when all the patient has to do is turn on the TV to hear that she will be heaped with scorn if she recovers, and with tributes if she gives in.

The cost of death's glamour is dead women—not only the ones we play on the jukebox and read about in the papers, but the hundreds or thousands whose names we don't know. We continue to fill the air with angelic dead girls and demonic sick people, with immortal suicides and washed-up old women. And when women die, we deny all responsibility: We loved them all along.

To forgive the dead, to immortalize the dead, is not forgiveness. It's one more sign of how impossible forgiveness is—of telling women that, once they've fallen, their punishment will never end. It is a way of telling a woman who breaks the rules that she cannot stand for long. That, sooner or later, the house always wins. Whatever you try, there are more of us than there are of you, and there is only one ending.

And that ending, of course, is another beginning. After we've buried the trainwreck, and forgiven her everything, we have to deal with the sad fact that she can't entertain us any more. The death of the trainwreck, and the orgy of public compassion that follows, is also just a very loud, noisy process of denial and distraction that takes place while the media trains its sights on the next lucky girl.

Part II

THE TRAINWRECK: HER OPTIONS

5

SHUT UP

Here's a serious question: When was the last time you, an average person and/or consumer of celebrity media, thought about Tara Reid?

If you're like most of us, it's probably been a while. Years, in fact. And yet, in the early 2000s, Reid was a genuine, no-fooling member of the A-list. She was a major player in the *American Pie* series, had a small but significant role in *The Big Lebowski,* and was cast in several major teen entertainments (*Josie and the Pussycats*, *Van Wilder,* something called *Urban Legend* that appears to be a horror film and is most notable today for its intensely *fin de siècle* cast of Reid, Jared Leto, and Rebecca "the Noxzema Girl" Gayheart). At the height of her reign as Youth Culture royalty, she was engaged to its fearsome God-Emperor, Carson Daly of *Total Request Live.*

When she fell, she fell hard. The Daly engagement ended. She began to be known as a "party girl," one of the era's many code words for "promiscuous" and "drunk." Reid leaned into this, hosting a new variant on *E!*'s night-life-around-the-world show *Wild On!*; it was called *Taradise*, it lasted for one year, and Reid would later say that it was "probably the stupidest thing I ever did . . . I didn't know it was going to ruin my career." Which was reasonable, because when other women had hosted a show with the same "go to a city, check out the nightclubs" premise, their careers had not in fact been ruined.

Humiliating as any of this may have been, it was also not the most personal or cruel reason that people had for hating her: By 2006, Tara Reid was mostly spoken about as a medical freak show, a collection of mutilated body parts and hideous scars. Her downfall came through a red-carpet "nip slip" (cousin to the "upskirt," the "nip slip" is the practice of taking semi-topless photos of a woman whose boob has popped out of her dress, under the pretext that breasts are inherently newsworthy), which revealed that her areola had been stretched out by breast implants.

"I was smiling like a fool and people were snapping away. When I realized it, I cried and begged the photographers not to print it, but it was everywhere," Reid said. "I was on the Web sites as having the ugliest boobs in the world."

Before long, stories about Reid's "botched" plastic surgery dominated all discussion of her. It wasn't just the breasts: Her stomach, which similarly had liposuction scars and looked a bit rippled (she says she had a hernia) was also the subject of vehement, widespread disgust.

These were relatively minor, human blemishes, the sort you would expect to find on a body formed of malleable flesh instead of heated, hormonal fantasy, but you wouldn't know it from reading about them; Reid was routinely framed as existing somewhere between Frankenstein's monster and the Elephant Man on the scale of medical anomaly. *CBS News* called Reid's breasts "deformed"; *People* ran a feature about whether Reid was "'moving on' from the botched breast augmentation and stomach liposuction that left her disfigured in 2004."

Reid was quoted in both those pieces. This was the final stop on her humiliation tour: She had to give interviews about her surgery, in which she publicly repented for the fact that she—a starlet, a sex symbol, a woman whose job it was to look thin and conventionally pretty—had gotten medical help to look thin and conventionally pretty.

"It wasn't really the pictures that hurt me. The comments hurt me. People wrote, 'Look at that flabby old actress,' 'She used to be so hot,' 'She's gross.' It's like, gosh, come on. I'm not fat," she told *People*. Predictably, the commenters of the world did not come flocking to Tara Reid's doorstep to offer heartfelt apologies. Perhaps more significant was the quote she gave *CBS News*, on how having a body that had become a national spectacle (old, freakish, blemished, *unsexy*) affected one's career as an actress who mostly played

young, beautiful seductresses. The surgery had only been
undertaken to help her career; she thought her breasts were
uneven, thought her stomach wasn't flat enough, and, well,
"I figured, I'm in Hollywood. I'm getting older. I'm going to
fix [it]." And yet, afterward:

"I couldn't wear a bikini," she said. "I lost a lot of work."

And that was it. At the peak of the Tara Reid Era, it
seemed that people would never stop talking about her. She
had ruled youth culture, as a sex symbol; she had ruled tabloid culture, as the epitome of ugliness. But when we ran
out of things to hate Tara Reid for, we stopped thinking
about her. After her body and personality had been rendered hyper-visible, invaded and dissected and ripped apart
in every way imaginable, in the end, Tara Reid just sort of . . .
disappeared.

Silence and invisibility are a familiar end point for celebrity trainwrecks. It's not just Tara Reid who vanished; the
same cycle repeated itself, even faster, for Vanessa Hudgens,
who was perhaps the most visible face of Disney's TV em-
pire next to Miley Cyrus, and the lynchpin of the hugely
popular *High School Musical* series, until her private nude
photos were leaked—she had taken them for her boyfriend;
someone else got hold of them, as "someone else" seems to
keep on doing—and she was dropped from the franchise.

Hudgens didn't even have a period of infamy and reality-
TV notoriety before we dropped her into the oubliette. She
had a much younger fan base; she was a Disney employee,

and therefore expected to be a model of sexless virtue; she was a woman of color, a biracial actress with a Filipina mother, whose sexuality was already more closely monitored, and more suspect, than the white and blond Reid (or, for that matter, Cyrus). Hudgens didn't get dragged around through the mud, as her white peers did; she simply went from ubiquitous to invisible, pretty much overnight.

These women still exist, and they still work in entertainment—Reid's presence is one of the recurring jokes of the *Sharknado* series, and Hudgens has grabbed roles in indie movies like *Spring Breakers*, where her acting has actually been fairly well received—but their star power has long since dissipated in a cloud of dirty jokes and negative headlines. Somehow, they just stopped being part of the conversation. Some women, like Britney Spears and Amanda Bynes, have their silence imposed upon them, by parental conservatorship. Even mainstays of the trainwreck industry, big attractions like Lindsay Lohan and Paris Hilton, have become less visible over time. The "fame" of a trainwreck is usually quick-burning; like a cat toying with a mouse, we trash these women for just as long as they have an entertaining amount of fight in them, and then, we get bored.

Yet this is not our first crop of disappearing girls. And the state of disgrace that befalls most celebrity trainwrecks—the metaphorical "disappearance" that comes with a sudden drop-off in fame—is actually not the worst thing that can happen to a woman. Alongside their stories, there is also a confusingly large number of female culture creators— smart, exceptional female artists, some of them actual geniuses—who have, quite literally, *disappeared*. As in, "from the face of the Earth."

Connie Converse, for example, has been called "the first American singer-songwriter." She lived in Greenwich Village in the 1950s, and recorded self-written ballads (often in her friends' living rooms) that borrowed heavily from folk and pop tradition, but skewed it toward sharp, often funny depictions of her own emotional landscape. It was the same approach that Bob Dylan and Leonard Cohen would become generational icons for adopting, but she did it in 1954, a decade before anyone had heard of either man. And it's a good thing she recorded those songs—and copyrighted them; her brother got the rights—because, by 1961, she believed she was a failure, and moved back home to Michigan, where she worked as a secretary. By 1973, she was depressed, and drinking heavily. And in 1974, she wrote a few letters to her family members saying that she wanted a fresh start, got into her car, and left town. She was never seen again. Her body of work was only discovered when a friend who'd recorded her in the '50s played a tape on a radio show. In 2004.

Somehow, that's not the only time a female genius's biography has ended with the woman in question evaporating into thin air. Consider the strange case of Barbara Newhall Follett, a child prodigy who published two critically acclaimed novels by the age of fourteen. The *Saturday Review of Literature* called her work "almost unbearably beautiful"; her book reviews (yep, she wrote those too) inspired H. L. Mencken to tell her parents that "you are bringing up the greatest critic we heard of in America." By the age of sixteen, her family had lost everything in the Great Depression, and she was working as a secretary. By twenty-three, she was in a rocky marriage; at twenty-five, she had a particularly bad argument with her husband, left the apartment carrying thirty dollars in cash, and (you guessed it) was never seen again.

In cases like Follett's and Converse's, one tends to expect the worst. (And one expects it, particularly, for Follett, whose husband did not report her missing for two weeks.) But these women didn't necessarily disappear into death. They may have simply disappeared into something even grimmer: everyday, anonymous existence.

Converse may have been the first female musician to disappear, but she's not the only one—indeed, she's not even the only one *in folk music*. Judee Sill was the Next Big Thing, a Laurel Canyon wunderkind who appeared on the cover of *Rolling Stone*; when she died of a drug overdose in 1979, her friends were shocked, largely because she'd gone missing so long ago that they'd assumed she was already dead. Shelagh McDonald recorded two popular folk albums, then disappeared until 2005, when she gave a brief interview to say that she'd been working in department stores and living on welfare; she had been so sure that her popularity would "burn out" that she never thought to pick up her royalty checks.

Then, there's Vashti Bunyan, a rising British pop star who went missing for the last three decades of the twentieth century. She only reappeared in 2000, due to the fact that her self-written 1970 album *Just Another Diamond Day*—a resounding critical and commercial failure at the time of its release—was considered a masterpiece, and was selling for around $2,000 per copy. None of which went to Bunyan, of course; she had no idea she had become famous until she Googled her own name. In the intervening time, she'd been a housewife. Her children knew *Diamond Day* existed, but were forbidden to listen to it in her presence; the failure had been so painful that Bunyan herself couldn't bear to hear the work that made her name.

Women disappear because they've been wrecked— because we've hated them for long enough to get bored of them. But they also disappear due to being misunderstood, or condescended to, or ignored. They vanish into irrelevance, but they also disappear into poverty, or addiction, or domesticity, or day jobs. The natural tendency is to see these disappearing girls as titillating unsolved mysteries. But they weren't spirited away to never-never land; they were talented professionals whose careers were put on hold for decades, or for the rest of their lives. And, in the face of the sheer number of stories like this, it's hard to interpret any one story as an individual tragedy or mystery.

The more reasonable explanation is that the historical lack of support for women as artists or public figures—the dismissal and condescension they face, the pressure to do the "reasonable" thing and put marriage and family first, the lack of cultural context that would make supporting and promoting them a political act—has resulted, not only in women avoiding the arts or being shamed out of them (*I confess, I do think*) but in a landscape where even relatively famous and ambitious women were so unimportant that they could disappear without a trace.

Which brings us to the idea that silence is not just an unlucky outcome, for a woman. It may be the natural outcome—as far as many people are concerned, the *ideal* outcome—of being female in a sexist world.

Which is to say: In the present day, silence may be the end of a famous woman's career. But in the story of women as a whole, silence has always been the *beginning*: The culturally prescribed and enforced mode of female life, the thing every woman's work had to fight through or around in order to exist. As Virginia Woolf put it, in her much-misquoted and much-bumper-stickered adage: "Anon, who wrote so many poems without signing them, was often a woman."

A Room of One's Own, of course, is a book entirely devoted to female silence; it sets out to answer the question of whether there *were* women in literature, and, if not, where they'd all gone. And, in that book, Woolf wrestled with the fact that the history of women's writing—one of the most permanent, and most obvious, ways that women have managed to make themselves heard in public—is also a history of women who have tried not to be noticed or seen as writers:

> *It was the relic of the sense of chastity that dictated anonymity to women even so late as the nineteenth century. Currer Bell, George Eliot, George Sand, all the victims of inner strife as their writings prove, sought ineffectively to veil themselves by using the name of a man. Thus they did homage to the convention, which if not implanted by the other sex was liberally encouraged by them (the chief glory of a woman is not to be talked of, said Pericles, himself a much-talked-of man) that publicity in women is detestable. Anonymity runs in their blood. The desire to be veiled still possesses them.*

All true. Brontë even said as much, counseling a friend who had the misfortune of having a musically gifted daughter: "I was told you had once some thoughts of bringing Fanny out as a professional singer, and it was added Fanny did not like the project . . . Fanny probably looks on publicity as degrading, and I believe for a woman it is degrading

if it is not glorious." A woman must be perfect, or not be
anything at all, to encounter fame without being shamed or
scarred.

Mary Beard, writing in the *London Review of Books*, traces
the idea as far back as the Odyssey: Telemachus, as a means
of claiming his manhood, tells Penelope to "go back up
into your quarters, and take up your own work, the loom
and the distaff . . . speech will be the business of men, all
men, and of me most of all." The word he uses, Beard tells
us, is important; gossip and informal conversation are not
denoted by it. The speech Telemachus is claiming for men
is *muthos*, speaking with authority in public. This speech is
also forbidden to women in Christian scripture: "Let the
woman learn in silence, with all subjection. But I suffer not
a woman to teach, nor to usurp authority over the man, but
to be in silence."

These injunctions against female speech were not just
cultural. They also passed into law. In Europe and the
United States, there were crimes of speech—like being a
"common scold," an "angry woman who, by brawling and
wrangling amongst her neighbours, disturbs the public
peace"—that only women could commit. Common scolds
were punished by being made to wear a gag called a "scold's
bridle" in public; it was made of metal, and sometimes lined
with blades or spikes, so that moving one's tongue at all
would cause injury. For those who felt that the bridle was
too cruel, there was also "ducking"—repeatedly submerg-

ing a woman in a lake or river, or (if all else failed) a horse trough, to simulate the feeling of drowning—which, as you may have already noticed, is basically identical to the punishment we call "waterboarding," and regard as a form of torture, in the present day. Don't worry, though: Common scold laws in the United States were ruled unconstitutional. After a New Jersey woman was successfully convicted of the offense in 1972.

It's no wonder, then, that we make such ugly, public sacrifices of women who've dared to become famous. The expansion required to make oneself heard or seen by the public—the act of *muthos*—is deeply at odds with the basic female work of getting and staying small.

And so it is that the history of women's written speech is littered with lacunae, dodges and feints around personal fame—women who've used male or androgynous pen names (Currer Bell, George Sand, George Eliot, J. K. Rowling) or who have relied on flat anonymity (Jane Austen's novels, published under the byline "A Lady"; Mary Shelley's *Frankenstein*, first published by "Anonymous"), or who simply didn't publish at all (Emily Dickinson, writing hundreds of poems and stuffing them in her desk drawer, where they stayed until her death). So it is that the "singer-songwriter" genre—the one art form that is pretty much explicitly dedicated to putting a person's voice and perspective out there, embodied and audible, in public—has such an odd habit of losing track of its female practitioners. So it is that women to this day attempt *muthos* with trepidation and tactical defenses. Here's Woolf again, and here's where she gets weird:

> *[Women] are not even now as concerned about the health*
> *of their fame as men are, and, speaking generally, will*
> *pass a tombstone or a signpost without feeling an irresist-*
> *ible desire to cut their names on it, as Alf, Bert or Chas.*
> *must do in obedience to their instinct, which murmurs if*
> *it sees a fine woman go by, or even a dog, Ce chien est*
> *a moi. And, of course, it may not be a dog, I thought,*
> *remembering Parliament Square, the Sieges Allee and*
> *other avenues; it may be a piece of land or a man with*
> *curly black hair.*

"It is one of the great advantages of being a woman," Woolf concludes with evident satisfaction, "that one can pass even a very fine negress without wishing to make an Englishwoman of her."

Of course, Woolf's reader may very well be a "negress." Who is also a woman. And for whom the innocence of white women, or their instinct to ownership, may be substantially more in doubt. In the midst of all these Georges and J.K.s and Anons, and in considering the tactical invisibility of "A Lady," it's instructive to remember at least one other pen name adopted to conceal an urgent truth. We could consider the account published in the *New York Tribune*, in April 1853, under the byline "A Fugitive Slave."

•

Anatomy of a Trainwreck

HARRIET JACOBS

"As this is the first time that I ever took my pen in hand to make such an attempt," she began, "you will not say that it is fiction, for had I the inclination I have neither the brain or talent to write it."

This was Harriet Jacobs's first published statement. She was a former slave, a fugitive from North Carolina, living in New York. Her brother John, who had also escaped, had become active in the abolitionist movement; one of his projects was an anti-slavery reading room, a library where documents on the cause could be found. Harriet had been allowed to read, growing up, before teaching slaves to read or write became illegal; she was allowed to use secondhand textbooks that had belonged to her owner. But her adult relationship to language began there, in the reading room, where she spent at least four days a week studying. Her first piece of published writing is a letter to her local paper, in response to the fact that former first lady Julia Tyler had written an editorial praising slavery's benefits to the American woman.

American women, and specifically enslaved American black women, were being raped. And Harriet Jacobs knew

it. She had seen it; she had barely escaped it. And despite being profoundly frightened of writing publicly—"I have not
the Courage to meet the criticism and ridicule of Educated
people," she claimed—she found herself remarkably able to
inform a first lady that she was full of shit:

"Would you not think that Southern Women had cause
to despise that Slavery which forces them to bear so much
deception practiced by their husbands?" she wrote.

> *Yet all this is true, for a slaveholder seldom takes a white
> mistress, for she is an expensive commodity, not as sub-
> missive as he would like to have her, but more apt to be
> tyrannical; and when his passion seeks another object, he
> must leave her in quiet possession of all the gewgaws that
> she has sold herself for. But not so with his poor slave
> victim, that he has robbed of everything that can make
> life desirable; she must be torn from the little that is left
> to bind her to life, and sold by her seducer and master,
> caring not where, so that it puts him in possession of
> enough to purchase another victim.*

This letter is, among other things, persuasive evidence
that Harriet Jacobs was a genius. She had never received
formal education; she had never received even informal education after the age of twelve. The *Tribune* added punctuation to her statement, because, in her earliest writing, she
avoided it: "the spelling I believe was every word correct

punctuation I did not attempt for I never studied Grammer there fore I know nothing about it," she explained. But her voice—long, elaborate, lyrical sentences, each one loaded with immense emotional charge—was there from the moment she put pen to paper. When she grabbed hold of language, she made it sing.

It was that very genius that wound up doing her in. Jacobs is a unique case, among all the women in this book. She was not publicly humiliated, not vilified, not forcibly exposed. But she was wrecked all right: faced wi th her story, and with her exceptional skill in telling it, the world just plain refused to believe that she existed at all. Until the 1970s, Harriet Jacobs—known mainly as "Linda Brent," the pen name she used for her autobiography, *Incidents in the Life of a Slave Girl*—was, in fact, believed to be a fictional character, invented by her white editor, Lydia Maria Child.

Historian John Blassingame gave a neat summary of all the reasons *Incidents* was "not credible":

> *The story is too melodramatic: miscegenation and cruelty, outraged virtue, unrequited love and planter licentiousness appear on practically every page. The virtuous Harriet sympathizes with her wretched mistress who has to look on all the mulattoes fathered by her husband, refuses to bow to the lascivious demands of her master, bears two children, and then runs away and hides in a garret in her grandmother's cabin for seven years until she*

*is able to escape to New York. In the meantime her white
lover has acknowledged his paternity of her children, pur-
chased their freedom, and been elected to Congress.*

Then, too, the book bore certain damning similarities
to women's popular fiction. Specifically, to *Uncle Tom's Cabin*
and *Jane Eyre*. In all three books, a young woman becomes
an object of sexual attention from the man she works for—
in Brontë's book, it's romantic; in Stowe's, it's prostitution;
in Jacobs's, it's threats of rape or murder. In both *Jane* and
Incidents, the heroine awakens to see that man's wife standing over her threateningly in the night. Bertha Rochester
awakes Jane, who passes out from fright; Linda becomes
the object of violent hatred and jealousy from "Mrs. Flint,"
who stands over her bed at night and whispers sexually sug-
gestive things to see if the sleeping Linda will confess to an
affair with her husband. All three books include a woman
being trapped in an attic: Bertha, Cassy, and Linda. Even
the ending of *Incidents* is seemingly a *Jane Eyre* reference:
"Reader, my story ends with freedom; not in the usual way,
with marriage," Jacobs wrote, flipping the script on one of
the most famous novels of her age.

And yet, it was all true. Even the attic. Even the rape
threats. Even the jealous, violent wife. The *Jane Eyre* and
Uncle Tom's Cabin references are there because, well, Jacobs
had probably read them both; she knew Stowe (though she
wound up not liking her) and her employer, Cornelia Wal-

lis, owned a copy of *Jane Eyre*. She specifically intended for her book to be read by privileged white women, whom she hoped to shock into political awareness. Jacobs would have been exercising good sense by studying the literature to figure out what her target audience liked, and fine technique in enlisting the reader's sympathies by recalling other beloved heroines. But what was literature, when written by white women who'd imagined it, was "melodrama" when written by a black woman who'd actually lived it.

Then there was the congressman. Who was also real, and who was perhaps the greatest obstacle to Jacobs, when it came time to write her story. After enduring years of sexual harassment, Jacobs had made one last, desperate bid to avoid being raped. She had slept, voluntarily, with the white son of one of the richest families in town. It worked: Once the affair became known, "Dr. Flint" (in reality, her master, Dr. James Norcom) backed off, at least physically. There were no consequences for raping or killing a slave, but there would certainly be social fallout from interfering with the affairs of a more powerful white man. Interpersonal awkwardness was more of a barrier to rape, for James Norcom, than a fifteen-year-old girl's pain.

In other words: Harriet's only escape from violence and coerced sex was another, slightly less violent form of coerced sex. And yet, she blamed herself. She was very nearly unable to speak of it, even to close friends.

"Though impelled by a natural craving for human sympathy, she passed through a baptism of suffering, even in recounting her trials to me, in private confidential conversations. The burden of these memories lay heavily upon her spirit," wrote Amy Post, the woman she eventually told. "[Her] sensitive spirit shrank from publicity . . . Even in talking with me, she wept so much, and seemed to suffer such mental agony, that I felt her story was too sacred to be drawn from her by inquisitive questions, and I left her free to tell as much, or as little, as she chose. Still, I urged upon her the duty of publishing her experience, for the sake of the good it might do; and, at last, she undertook the task."

To Amy, Harriet explained the burden of silence on her: "Dear Amy if it was the life of a Heroine with no degradation associated with it . . . your purity of heart and kindly sympathies won me at one time to speak of my children it is the only words that has passed my lips since I left my Mothers door I had determined to let others think as they pleased but my lips should be sealed and no one had a right to question me for this reason when I first came North I avoided the Antislavery people as much as possible because I felt that I could not be honest and tell the whole truth."

Post's description of Jacobs's pain sounds like what we would now call post-traumatic stress disorder. And, honestly, how could she *not* have had it? She had lived with the threat of rape, torture, or death, for both herself and her children, for years. She had seen it. Even when she escaped, she had spent seven years in a crawl-space the size of a spacious coffin; she was unable to sit, stand, or turn over without bumping her head on the ceiling, unable to see the outside world except through peepholes that she had made in the walls, and her movement was constricted to such an extent that, at one point, her legs just stopped working. Her unwillingness or inability to speak, or her inability to relive the events in question without agony, seems like the only possible outcome for a woman emerging from decades of unremitting trauma.

Presumably it also had something to do with the sheer size of her task, the fatal nature of the truth she had to impart. The Cult of True Womanhood was at its height in Jacobs's lifetime; the belief in the delicate, angelic, asexual nature of women, and of the sanctity of marriage, motherhood, and domesticity, was so widespread that even feminists were using it to advocate their cause. And Jacobs had to say that it was a lie. That it was only tenable because millions of women—black women—*were not allowed* chastity, or delicacy, or protection. While white women's sexuality was being written out of existence, black women and girls were completely unprotected from sexual predation. The men preaching the sanctity of marriage and motherhood were building a business out of rape and the selling their own children. What Harriet Jacobs had to say struck at the foundations of the deeply racist American patriarchy. And she had to say it, while also admitting that she had survived the worst of it. That she, too, had never been allowed to be a True Woman.

"Pity me, and pardon me, O virtuous reader!" Jacobs eventually wrote, on the matter of the congressman.

> *You never knew what it is to be a slave; to be entirely unprotected by law or custom; to have the laws reduce you to the condition of a chattel, entirely subject to the will of another. You never exhausted your ingenuity in avoiding the snares, and eluding the power of a hated tyrant; you never shuddered at the sound of his footsteps, and trembled within hearing of his voice. I know I did wrong. No one can feel it more sensibly than I do. The painful and humiliating memory will haunt me to my dying day. Still, in looking back, calmly, on the events of my life, I feel that the slave woman ought not to be judged by the same standard as others.*

This explanation—careful, diplomatic, sometimes flat-out self-abasing, but ultimately unapologetic—was what made it to the book. Because she did tell the truth. Eventually, somehow, she did make herself revisit that trauma, and share it. She changed all the names, including her own; there's no evidence that she feared capture (a white friend had "bought" her from Norcom eventually, essentially paying him off to leave her alone, a concession to slavery's legality that Jacobs found immensely painful and humiliating) but she did make that one self-protective dodge. And no one would listen, even then.

She first spoke to Harriet Beecher Stowe, to see if she would consider serving as a ghostwriter; Stowe wrote to Jacobs's white employer to "verify" her account of sexual harassment and exploitation, seemingly neither knowing nor caring that Jacobs considered this to be sensitive information, and had never disclosed it to her boss. Jacobs wrote the book herself, without a ghostwriter, and publishers told her it would not be salable without the endorsement of a major author like Harriet Beecher Stowe. She got recognized activist Lydia Maria Child to edit it (Child would say "I don't think I changed fifty words in the whole volume") and, when they'd sold it to a publisher, the publisher went out of business before printing it. She used her own money to buy back the printing plates, paid a Boston house to print it, and sold the fucking thing by hand—the woman who'd been physically incapable of talking about her trauma, selling an account of it to people who had to look her in the face before buying—and then the Civil War began, and there was something else to talk about.

Incidents went out of print. Harriet disappeared. She wrote articles, she worked in activist circles, she worked in refugee camps, she ran a school for freed slaves. She identified herself, publicly, as the "Linda" of *Incidents*. She knew Frederick Douglass. She knew Elizabeth Cady Stanton, whose racism eventually drove her out of the feminist movement. Still, her most prominent mention in the history of nineteenth-century literature or activism was a half-sentence from Stanton, using the wrong name and referring to her in the same breath as a fictional character: "The brave deeds of Margaret Garner, Linda Brent and Mrs. Stowe's Eliza."

So she became Linda. And she became unreal. She became Lydia Maria Child's melodramatic invention. For all the silence she'd fought through, for all the shame and lack of confidence she'd found a way to work around, it ultimately didn't matter: Silence was imposed on her by the world. And then, in the 1970s, scholar Jean Fagan Yellin got curious about *Incidents*. She looked into the archive of an activist quoted in the book, Amy Post. Suddenly, into the world came the letters of a woman who did not think she could write. Long, lyrical sentences, a voice you could recognize right away. Suddenly, where there had been only fiction, there was Harriet Jacobs.

What's striking about Harriet Jacobs's silence is that, in some ways, she sounds just like anyone. The levels of atrocity she saw and endured are unimaginable. She's even clear, in her book, that some part of her pain may be unimaginable: No matter how open she is in telling her life story, she also tells us that no one can really *know* what she's endured unless they have also been enslaved. And yet, when Jacobs demurs and protests that she doesn't have it in her to write—that she can't take criticism, that she's not educated, that she's not a real heroine, that she'd need to be more sympathetic to be worthy of a hearing—she sounds like any other woman I've known refusing to push herself out into the world.

But silence from within is not the whole story. Her silence was also practically, even legally, mandated by the culture she lived in. No one faced a higher, harder barrier to public speech than Jacobs did. For most of her life, she was legally barred from choosing a career, voting, deciding where to live, or even reading, let alone writing. Her silence was shared by millions of other women who were literally rendered property, whose bodies and suffering were commodified in the most literal and brutal way possible. They were seen, used, harmed, killed, but not heard. Because to make themselves heard would be to make themselves human.

Harriet Jacobs was able to break that silence—she was able to respond to Julia Tyler. It was an audacious act. But it was also a moment when the safety afforded by silence was outweighed by the threat of not speaking. Tyler was telling the world that slavery was good for women; Tyler was wrong; if Jacobs didn't say something, it was entirely possible that Tyler would get to *keep* being wrong, and make the world wrong in her image.

Which is to say, Jacobs was able to get to the other side of silence by realizing exactly what makes it insupportable: If you don't tell people who you are and what you know, other people will be able to tell the world who you are *for* you. And, if it pleases them, they will be able to lie.

Of course, Jacobs also experienced silence's cruelest

trick: Even if you do convince yourself to speak, someone else has to agree to listen to you. If they deny you, silence comes back. And it will swallow you whole.

•

In the early twenty-first century, the ban on women's public speech has seemingly been broken. Women are best-selling authors, world leaders, singer-songwriters, film directors, TED Talk–givers; women, even when they have accomplished none of the above, are typically connected to social media platforms like Twitter or Facebook, which allow them to broadcast their written speech (or, in the case of YouTube videos, their *actual* speech) to a national or international audience. It is easy to assume that the fight is over; that women can take their right to a voice for granted.

Easy, but unwise. Even now, there are strange discrepancies and imbalances in women's public speech as compared to men's. We hear, for example, about "imposter syndrome," the strangely common belief among high-achieving women that they don't actually deserve any of their success. We also hear about the "confidence gap," the fact that women are statistically far less likely to apply for jobs or ask for raises than men are. In politics, this is called the "ambition gap," and it supposedly accounts for the fact that men are vastly overrepresented in government; men are 80 percent of the U.S. Congress, and only 49 percent of the U.S. population. One 2001 study found that women are twice as likely as men to say they are "not at all qualified" to run for political office—and that men are 60 percent more likely to rate themselves as "very qualified" to do so.

Then, there are the everyday aggressions that women report when exercising their voices. There is the Internet-neologized phenomenon of "mansplaining" (a man explaining something to a woman that she already knows, sometimes better than he does). There is the strange fact that women's actual voices tend to be viewed as somehow more objectionable than men's. Women are also stereotyped as the more talkative gender, despite the fact that research suggests men talk more than women do; when men and women are deliberately given equal speaking time at a public event or discussion, the women are perceived to have talked *more* than the men, simply because equally distributed speech is so rare that it still feels somehow unnatural.

Speech will be the business of men, all men, and of me in particular: Scratch the surface, and plenty of men are still willing to believe or repeat that millennia-old declaration. And, puzzlingly, women are still likely to agree with them. On some basic level, silence is still the default state of female existence. Though the world has changed to the point that we can no longer prevent women from speaking—women are technically *allowed* to read, write, hold jobs, get into an argument with the neighbors without being waterboarded for it—there are still many, many ways that the world convinces women to steal speech from themselves.

Enforcing silence is easy. All you have to do is make it feel like the safest option. You can, for example, make speaking as unpleasant as possible, by creating an anonymous social media account to flood women with virulent personal criticism, sexual harassment, and threats. You can talk over women, or talk down to them, until they begin to doubt that they have anything worthwhile to say. You can encourage men's speech, and ignore women's, so that women will get the message that they are taking up too much room, and contributing too little value. You can nitpick a woman's actual voice—the way she writes, her grammar, her tone, her register, her accent—until she honestly believes she's bad at talking, and spends more time trying to sound "better" than thinking about what she wants to say.

And if a woman somehow makes it past all this, you can humiliate her anyway. It's easy to bemoan the gaps in women's confidence, or women's ambition; to blame women for being afraid to make themselves heard. But, if women believe they have more to lose than men from being visible, they're right. They do. Success, or even the visible attempt to succeed, is in fact dangerous for women. And after a lifetime spent in trainwreck culture—a life spent watching the most beautiful, lucky, wealthy, successful women in the world reduced to deformed idiot hags in the media, and battered back into silence and obscurity through the sheer force of public disdain—women may not be able to see "being heard" as a good thing in itself. We understand, on some

level, that success can be a gateway to another, more profound, more painful kind of failure.

We never stopped publicly exhibiting the mentally ill for
titillation. We never stopped punishing mouthy women. Silence is still seductive, and still enforced. Until that changes,
our history will be littered with blank spaces and disappearing acts—not only the girls who fell silent, or the girls who
vanished, but the women who were never there at all.

6

SPEAK UP

In June 2007, Britney Spears published a blog post (title: "You'll Never See It My Way, Because You're Not Me") asking her fans to choose the title of her new album. Here were the candidates:

Dignity

Down Boy

Integrity

OMG Is Like Lindsay Lohan OK Like

What If the Joke Is on You

The album wound up being called *Blackout*. In a classic Spears Management Move—presenting something incredibly scandalous, while staunchly maintaining ignorance of any scandalous implications—Jive Records claimed that the title "[referred] to blocking out negativity and embracing life fully."

That was not what *Blackout* meant, and everyone damn well knew it. The album was released at the peak of Spears's trainwreck narrative—after her first rehab stay, after she shaved her head, after her divorce, after that fatal umbrella—and that of several other women. The *MTV News* post that listed the potential album titles also mentioned that Lohan was being sued for crashing into a parked van while driving drunk, and that Paris Hilton had been released from the medical ward at the Twin Towers Correctional Facility, where she was serving time for her own DUI. Three weeks before *Blackout* was released, Hilton appeared on David Letterman, where he ritually humiliated her by refusing to ask her about anything other than her prison time. ("I don't really want to talk about it any more," Hilton protested weakly. "This is where you and I are different," Letterman said, grinning from ear to ear, "because this is *all* I want to talk about.") In a year when the country cared about nothing more than punishing party girls, Spears was releasing an album named after binge drinking.

Which is to say, she was talking about it. She'd been talking about it for quite some time—in 2004, she and her label had evidently scrapped an album entitled *Original Doll*; one of the only surviving tracks was "Mona Lisa," which contained the lyrics "Now see everyone's watching / As she starts to fall / They want her to break down / And be a legend of a fall"—and she was by now committed to going on the offensive. One of the singles, "Piece of Me" (the songwriters claimed that they submitted it in violation of "an unwritten rule that no songs should be about Britney's life"), was nothing more nor less than a recap of Britney Spears's press narrative to date, beginning with "I'm Miss American Dream since I was seventeen" and continuing through "get in line with the paparazzi who's flipping me off / hoping I'll resort to some havoc, end up settling in court." The video featured Spears seducing anonymous men in public bathrooms and dancing around on-screen tabloid headlines.

It's a strange thing to realize, if your memory of that time (like mine) is of Spears, Lohan, and Hilton being subject to unremitting and unanimous hatred. But the Britney Spears Trainwreck Narrative always had a counterpoint, and it was coming from Britney Spears.

The story of the twentieth century is, in some ways, a story of women getting louder.

On some level, this is a technological thing. By the 1920s, we had movies, and recorded music, and radio—all the core elements of a celebrity-industrial complex. By the 1950s, we had the complex, and the industries devoted to covering it: Movie magazines, tabloids, gossip columns,

television. As the century wound to a close, our powers of
surveillance were astonishing: twenty-four-hour news channels, reality TV, fan sites, chat boards, and the beginnings
of blogs, which would soon change everything about how
trainwrecks were made. The sheer number of ways to pub-
licize your mistakes—or, if you were unlucky, to have them
publicized—escalated almost unthinkably far and fast over
the course of eighty years. When Mary Wollstonecraft was
being demolished, her critics couldn't even publish an unflattering photo of her. If you wanted to call someone a slut,
you had to resort to poetry. But by the time Britney showed
up, the wonders of science had provided us with dozens or
hundreds of ways to make her look like an asshole.

So, women became louder in part because, over the
course of the twentieth century, everyone became louder.
We gained—and are still gaining—vastly more access to
the lives of total strangers, and that meant that women with
public lives and careers had to develop new ways to defend
themselves in the court of public opinion.

By the time Spears released *Blackout*, she was joining a
long pop tradition of the "You Don't Know Me" song: Back
when Billie Holiday was working the redemption circuit,
she was peppering her catalogue with songs about the evils
of gossip ("Don't Talk About Me When I'm Gone," " 'Taint
Nobody's Business If I Do") so that her live shows could
deliver elegant, subtly virtuosic variations on the message
"kindly shut the fuck up about my drug use." In 1992, Whit-

ney Houston answered the scandalized questions about her marriage to Bobby Brown—why America's squeaky-clean pop sweetheart was getting tangled up with a known drug user—by releasing a duet with him. It was entitled "Something in Common," and opened with Brown announcing that the song "is dedicated to those who don't believe in real love, especially our love." The title phrase was repeated so many times that it stopped sounding like a hook, and started sounding like an attempt at mass brainwashing: *We have something in common. We have something in common.* **We have something in common.** *Yes we do.* Taylor Swift did the same thing with "Blank Space," in 2014; it was possibly the best-received single of her career, and effectively halted the "Swift is a crazy ex-girlfriend" narrative in its tracks.

But maybe it's a mistake to start with self-defense. The statements cited above are largely denials and disavowals, statements of *I am not* rather than *I am, and this is how it is.* And yet, in order for those women to publicly respond to the narratives about their lives, they had to have public lives in the first place—possible, in part, because the world had changed around them. Brace yourself, Reader. For I am about to un-ironically utter the phrase "consciousness-raising."

It's a weird little term, isn't it? It makes you feel square and older than you thought you were, like going to the mall to pick out a sensible pantsuit. It has the unmistakable fug of the '70s all over it: Just saying the phrase aloud seems to

summon an air of un-ironic goddess-invoking, and hand-
written cookbooks with a lot of material about lentils, and
spelling it *womyn*, with the "y." I always hear the tender,
acoustic strains of womyn's folk music in my head when
I say it; I also, for some reason, envision handmade quilts.
Which is all to say that "consciousness-raising," as a concept
or feminist tactic, has largely been relegated to that quilt-
infested realm of the feminine and quaint: It seems to derive
from, and chiefly appertain to, a world where young radicals
were not yet worldly or jaded enough to be automatically
creeped out by communes.

And yet, it is not so. "Consciousness-raising" was not
only a powerful radical strategy, it's perhaps the most rele-
vant and enduring legacy of second-wave feminism. Beginning in the late 1960s, in radical feminist collectives such as
the New York Radical Women and Redstockings, women
began to sit down with each other, and take turns honestly
answering each other's questions. Here, from a 1971 guide
to starting your own group, were some of the questions:

- *Why did you marry the man you did? (or date the man
  you do?)*
- *What was your first sex experience?*
- *Do you pretend to have an orgasm?*
- *Have you had an abortion?*
- *What do you feel about lesbianism? What do you know
  about it?*

I think that last question may be my favorite, simply because it sounds so very "have you heard of our Lord and Savior Jesus Christ." And, indeed, one of the many benefits of second-wave feminism was that it allowed and encouraged women to undertake independent study upon that matter. But then, perhaps most crucially, there was this one:

- *What is a "nice girl"? Were you a "nice girl"?*

This was the question that the feminist movement generally, and the consciousness-raising groups specifically, were out to answer. Not simply how to make the world better for women, but who women actually *were*: What they thought, what they felt, what they went through, and how very far it deviated from the established patriarchal script.

For some women, the project was purely pragmatic. In her essay on consciousness-raising, for example, Kathie Sarachild mentions the struggle over how to establish women's intelligence. One colleague wanted to find the proof in studies, summon up the necessary facts and figures. But for Sarachild, that was a lost cause: "For every scientific study we quote, the opposition can find their scientific studies to quote . . . We know from our own experience that women play dumb for men because, if we're too smart, men won't like us. I know, because I've done it. We've all done it. Therefore, we can simply deduce that women are smarter than men are aware of[.]"

We know how to prioritize what social-justice types call "lived experience" now, and so it's easy to forget how radical these statements really were. There were precedents— critics were quick to point out that consciousness-raising was suspiciously similar to the Maoist practice of "speaking bitterness"—but, in a world where women were mostly encouraged to focus on relationships with men, and to say mostly what those men wanted to hear, the mere fact of women talking to one another uninhibitedly, and regarding themselves and each other as credible sources on important subjects, was immensely strange. Feminist approaches like Sarachild's put forth a new methodology—*we know from our own experience; I know, because I've done it*—which rejected science, medicine, philosophy, and most of literature in order to argue that the only real "authorities" on womanhood were women. And not "special," accomplished, or even particularly educated women: In this paradigm, women gained "expert" status simply by being female.

That was it. That was all it took to have more expertise than, say, Sigmund Freud. If you were a woman, and your experience suggested that Freud was wrong about vaginal orgasms—he thought you'd start having them once you accepted your role as a woman—and if you could talk to enough women whose orgasms suggested likewise, well, then, *Freud was fucking wrong.* And that was that. One of the leading theories of human sexuality, demolished in a few hours, simply by virtue of the fact that you'd talked about your sex life.

Advocates of consciousness-raising were quick to point out that their methodology was not unscientific. ("Our meetings were called coffee klatches, hen parties or bitch sessions," Sarachild writes. "We responded by saying, 'Yes, bitch, sisters, bitch.'") The preferred procedure, for most groups, was to give each woman present the chance to answer a question, before moving on to the next question or discussion, and to remain (if at all possible) non-judgmental. This wasn't for sisterly, kumbaya-singing reasons—women in these radical groups wound up hating each other as often as anyone else—but for the purpose of producing accurate data. You didn't want to know how any particular woman felt, but how many women felt the same way, and you didn't want to shut anyone down, because it would interfere with the flow of information.

And yet, the very nature of that intimacy could not help but open doors for particular and individual women. The best way forward for women, according to consciousness-raising, was to speak: bluntly, explicitly, very personally, and in the presence of someone who could hear you. You had to drop all the hiding, all the insecurity, and just claim your own narrative in your own words. It not only changed the agenda of the movement; it changed the participants' ideas of themselves.

"As a movement woman, I've been pressured to be strong, selfless, other-oriented, sacrificing, and in general pretty much in control of my own life," wrote Carol Hanisch, in her own landmark essay on the topic (it's entitled "The Personal Is Political," and yes, that phrase stuck around). "It is at this point a political action to tell it like it is, to say what I really believe about my life instead of what I've always been told to say."

And while the feminists of the 1960s and 1970s rejected the idea that what they were doing was a form of "therapy," they also felt clear on what the consequences of *not* doing it would be: "In the absence of feminist activity," Cathy Levine wrote in her defense of consciousness-raising, "women take tranquilizers, go insane, and commit suicide."

Despite all the talk of collectivity, that is one strikingly specific vision. And it likely has its roots in one or two very specific stories, about what a woman's oppression looked like, and where it might lead. Before the 1970s, before the formation of the radical collectives, before consciousness-raising, there was simply the consciousness, recorded on paper, of the former Mrs. Ted Hughes.

•

Anatomy of a Trainwreck

SYLVIA PLATH

The story of Sylvia Plath begins with her death. She committed suicide in the winter of 1963, shortly after writing the best work of her life. By the time those books were published—*Ariel,* in 1965; *The Bell Jar,* first released under her own name in 1971—she had been gone for years. She couldn't speak for the work, or explain it, or defend it. Perhaps most crucially, she could not make any decisions as to where, how, or in what form it was published. This was where the fight began.

The eruption of Plath into the American public consciousness can most likely be traced to the publication of "Daddy" in *Time* magazine, in 1966. She was already a well-regarded literary figure, especially after *Ariel,* but *Time* made her a star. Next to the poem, and a selection of photos, they described how "a pretty young mother of two children was found in a London flat with her head in the oven." Then, in heavy-breathing prose, *Time* promised "a strange and terrible poem she had written in her last sick slide toward suicide," calling Plath a "dragon who in her last months of life breathed a river of bile across the literary landscape."

Within the space of a few paragraphs, *Time* magazine had managed to transform Sylvia Plath from Betty Crocker into Godzilla. But then there was the poem itself. The rough beast that stomped its way toward Tokyo to be born: "Daddy, I have had to kill you," it declaimed, in lurching, inexorable rhythm, and racked up the body count from there: "A man in black with a Meinkampf look / and a love of the rack and the screw / and I said, I do, I do . . . If I've killed one man, I've killed two."

She didn't sound like a pretty young homemaker. "Daddy" was like an electrical line that snapped and landed on the family driveway. It hissed and writhed and gave off beautiful sparks, and trying to grab it with bare hands would end you. "Daddy" seethed; it threatened. It was decisively not a delicate, feminine utterance of melancholy, not the work of some flower-garlanded Ophelia floating passively downstream. Plath sounded angry enough to kill *somebody*, to be certain, but—in "Daddy," anyway—she wasn't on that list.

So who was? Not just Dad: The vampire husband, the torturous screw, the Meinkampf looker? What did he *do*?

It wasn't idle curiosity. Plath died six days before Betty Friedan's *The Feminine Mystique* was first published. The *Time* article was published in the same year as Valerie Solanas's first essay. By 1968, two years after "Daddy's" appearance in *Time*, the New York Radical Women would be marching on the Miss America pageant; that same year, dissidents who found Friedan and her NOW organization too conservative would converge with Valerie, and make her shooting of Andy into a *cause célèbre*. Plath had released a poem of rage against husbands and fathers—a poem that identified husbands and fathers with brutality, with violence, with *oppression*—at precisely the moment that American women were ready to rage against the sexist men in their lives.

And Sylvia had an advantage: Unlike Valerie, she was not living on the margins. She had published a book before her death, had studied with Robert Lowell, had given readings for the BBC, was a "real" writer with real credentials. "Confessional" writing itself was even a respected form, albeit one practiced largely by men like Lowell. Being white, straight, middle-class, a housewife, a mother, a good girl from a good college: All of these made her seem "representative" (at least, according to one very limiting definition of "representative"—which, to be fair, was the definition plenty of second-wave feminists used) and made her death seem like more than an isolated tragedy or an aberration in the pattern. And so, the groundswell of female anger underneath Sylvia, and the ways she resembled the American ideal, turned "Daddy" from a poem into an anthem.

And when the details became clear—that Plath's husband was a poet named Ted Hughes; that he had cheated on her while she was nursing their infant son; that she had kicked him out; that, because she had died before the divorce was finalized, and left no will, he controlled the publication of her work and received the profits from it—well, that anger had a very convenient place to go.

"I accuse / Ted Hughes," wrote Robin Morgan, in her poem "The Arraignment." Specifically, she accused him of wife-beating and murder. As out-of-line as these accusations seem now, with five intervening decades of proof against them, Morgan also wrote a few things that were harder to deny. Namely, that Hughes was making "a mint / by becoming Plath's posthumous editor."

Hughes threatened to sue. All copies of the offending book, *Monster*, were eventually pulled from Great Britain. This, it turned out, was where the rage against Hughes really originated: He kept a choke hold on any public utterance about Plath. If a friend published a two-part memoir of Plath's final days in the *Observer*, Hughes would make sure the second part got pulled. If a biographer wanted to quote her substantially, her estate—Hughes and his sister Olwyn, who disliked Plath in life and didn't get any fonder of her after death—would dictate Hughes-friendly rewrites before giving permission. And the people forbidden by Hughes to publish material about Sylvia Plath included, crucially, Sylvia Plath herself. *Ariel* came out—but Hughes had changed the order of poems and omitted some "personally aggressive" ones. Her journals were released—but Hughes admitted to burning or losing the ones from the last months of her life, and the edited versions were full of [OMISSION] marks. *The Bell Jar* was published—but Plath's second novel, about a woman facing the dissolution of her marriage, managed to get "lost" as well, one more glaring [OMISSION] in what had come to be a highly suspicious list.

Hughes was not evil. He grieved Plath, and suffered greatly: Assia Wevill, the woman for whom he left Plath, committed suicide herself a few years later, and killed their daughter as well. And, in all the censoring he did, he may have genuinely been trying to protect Sylvia's reputation. When her unedited journals were published, in 1999, it turned out the most suspicious [OMISSION] marks weren't hiding confessions of Hughes's brutality, as many initially suspected; they were hiding Plath's complaints about Ted's personal hygiene. He hadn't beaten her, he just didn't want the world to know how rarely he showered.

If anything, Hughes is best seen in the context of another grieving husband: Where William Godwin's response to Wollstonecraft's unexpected death had been to publish everything, no matter how potentially scandalous it was, Hughes's response was to withhold or destroy anything questionable, no matter how potentially scandalous it wasn't. Two widowers took precisely opposite routes, and wound up in the same disgrace: In the age of women's silence, unguarded speech was shameful. But in the age of women's speech, male-imposed silence was intolerable.

The banning of "The Arraignment" was the last straw, the moment when Hughes's controlling behavior came smack up against a political movement devoted to opposing male control. Feminists began to publish bootleg copies of "The Arraignment." His readings were picketed, by women whose placards frequently bore lines from Morgan's poem; sometimes women would stand up, during a lull in the reading, and begin to recite "The Arraignment" aloud. He began to cancel readings, for fear of disruption. By trying to make Morgan's poem disappear, he'd turned it into a cause.

Meanwhile, Plath's work kept coming. (And it was, to be clear, Hughes who let it come.) Her first novel, *The Bell Jar* was, if possible, an even more serendipitous work than *Ariel*. It was a blunt, witty, unsparing account of her first suicide attempt. It was also the tale of a girl who thought marriage would let a man "flatten [her] out under his feet," who could get into Honors English but was still confounded by the sexual double standard, who was subjected to attempted rape when she did try to express herself sexually, and who would frankly rather kill herself than work at a ladies' magazine and go without birth control. Everything second-wave feminists were ready to address, Plath had already talked about, simply by talking about herself. She had hung it out there, for God and all to see, and it wasn't simply ranting and raving and pornography. It was the problem of an age, of thousands or millions of girls like her. When women spoke, it seemed, they really did start to say all the same things.

And so, Plath became a prophet, and a martyr, someone who had seen the problems before she had a feminist movement to help her fix them, and who had died in part because feminism arrived too late. Like Valerie, she was a cautionary case, someone whose life story meant what the observer's politics needed it to mean. But, unlike Valerie, she had neither a criminal record nor the ability to disagree with her interpreters. She was more useful to her allies than to her enemies. She became the prototype of the woman who, in the absence of feminist activity, took tranquilizers, went insane, and committed suicide. Hughes's name began to disappear from Plath's gravestone. Over and over, "Sylvia

Plath Hughes" was chiseled away, until only "Sylvia Plath" remained. No one ever came forward to admit doing it; no one has ever given the reasons. It could have been an act of malice. It could have been a statement of her independent status as a writer: "Sylvia Hughes" didn't write those books, after all. Or it could have been one last, cruelly sarcastic [OMISSION] mark. He destroyed her journal. They destroyed his name.

I don't envy Hughes what he went through in the years after Plath's death. And I sincerely doubt that we can solve the problem of trainwrecks—of our gruesome appetite to see women suffer, or to see them punished for violating our ideas of how women "ought" to behave—by simply wrecking more men. But Plath was never invulnerable to the wrecking process.

There have been many attempts, over the years, to paint Plath back into a more familiar picture of sexual and emotional excess: "Sexually predatory, rabidly ambitious, mentally unstable," as a review of one Ted Hughes biography calls her. Where feminists saw a prophet, Hughes partisans saw a raving, fame-hungry succubus. August critic Harold Bloom sniffed that her poem "Lady Lazarus" was merely a "tantrum," and that Plath herself was just a fad: "Hysterical insanity, whatever its momentary erotic appeal, is not an affect that endures in verse." It's rare that a mere fad is important enough to merit a book-length takedown, but that seems to have escaped Bloom's notice.

Other writers have followed Bloom's lead, characterizing Plath's work (and, particularly, the poems in *Ariel*) as purely a symptom of her mental illness: Transcribed delusions, or else compulsive and insane acts of violence against the people in her life, committed through the unlikely medium of verse. Her work has been framed as a disease. And, in the cultural attempt to figure out precisely *which* mental illness can magically force someone to write two massively popular and enduring books, Plath has been posthumously diagnosed with psychotic depression, bipolar disorder, overly strong PMS, and at least two different personality disorders. One *PsychCentral* article on narcissistic personality disorder and motherhood opens with a Plath quote, noting that "[there] is a special place in hell for narcissistic mothers. Ms. Plath herself indulged in the ultimate narcissistic act when she committed suicide by sticking her head in the oven while her two young children were asleep in the same apartment." (If suicide is a narcissistic act, it seems oddly unlikely to benefit the narcissist in question.) And then there's this, from a 2003 article in the *Journal of the Royal Society of Medicine*, which diagnoses Plath with borderline personality disorder:

> *Plath's poetry can be seen to be preoccupied with 'border-line' themes (loss, violence, and contradictory experiences of the self) but these do not necessarily generate poetry.*

> *The association of instability with creativity is probably linked with another borderline trait, the capacity for intense concentration. This represents a dissociation from current surroundings and preoccupations, even when these are difficult, as they were when she was writing* Ariel.

No one would suggest that Plath wasn't mentally ill. Suicide is never a sign of radiant health. But this is another instance of the David Foster Wallace Conundrum: We say that David Foster Wallace was a genius (because he wrote *Infinite Jest*) and that he was also mentally ill (because he hanged himself). Even if his experience of mental illness substantially informed his writing (*Infinite Jest*, like *The Bell Jar*, is drawn largely from the author's experiences after a suicide attempt in college; the addiction-recovery center Wallace fictionalizes was his first stop after McLean, which also happened to be the exact same hospital Plath stayed in, and that she fictionalized in *The Bell Jar*), his writing isn't a symptom of his illness, but evidence of his ability to transcend it. But for Plath, even the most basic part of writing, the fact that she could sit down and concentrate long enough to compose a poem—the same skill displayed by every third-grader who has ever successfully completed a book report—is supposedly a form of madness. Men have problems. Women *are* problems.

Here we are again.

•

The promise of Plath's work was that a woman could de-fang the charges of hysteria by owning them. Unlike Sola-nas, who seemingly never saw herself as flawed or sick, or Wollstonecraft and Brontë, who swept their flaws under the carpet so as not to compromise themselves, or even Jacobs, who was honest, but played a delicate game of apologizing for "sins" that were not her fault so as to reach her audience, Plath took her own flaws as her subject, and thereby made them the source of her authority. By detailing her own over-abundant inner life, no matter how huge and frightening it was—her sexuality, her suicidality, her broken relation-ships, her anger at the world or at men—she could, in some crucial way, own that part of her story, simply because she chose to tell it. And, if she could do this, other women could do it, too.

It's true that, for all that has been written against her, and for all the writing we never got to see, Plath's ownership of her story gives her a measure of power. She could never be easily or completely slotted into the existing archetypes of crazy ex-girlfriend, half-dressed and hysterical Louise Augustine, or sexually voracious dirty girl, simply because we always have access to her own, complicated, individ-ual story. We can still read "Daddy" and feel the hissing electrical voltage of her disillusionment rising through the page. We can still read *The Bell Jar*—the smirk of nice-boy Buddy Willard when she breaks her leg shortly after reject-ing his marriage proposal, the "woman-hater" who calls her "slut" after he tries to rape her—and see exactly why being a young woman, trying to obtain some sexual satisfaction, is a frightening and dangerous thing. For all the diagnoses and interpretations, she remains ferociously herself; her voice is too strong to disappear inside some generalization about madwomen. The love her readers had for her voice was proven by their anger at even well-intentioned attempts to limit it, their insistence that the world deserved to hear everything Plath had to say.

But that love has never been taken entirely seriously. Nor does declaring Plath your favorite author win you many points in lit-nerd circles. At the beginning of Plath's fame, her fans were stereotyped as rabid, violent feminists. But, as early as 1979 and *Annie Hall*, the stereotypes were getting younger, drippier, and dumber: Woody Allen called her an "interesting poetess whose tragic suicide was misinterpreted as romantic by the college girl mentality." (Woody Allen, of course, being an infamously unreliable authority on what young girls enjoy.) Reading her was always gendered, and trivialized, but it got more trivial and more divorced from the political context as time went on. Now, consciousness-raising groups are hokey lentil talk, autobiographical writing is preferably done with a certain cool MFA-enabled distance, and Plath fans are mostly stereotyped as moody, melodramatic, self-absorbed teenage girls. Not exactly a glorious legacy.

If the movement for the feminist first-person has any

legacy at all, it has leaked down, out of the lofty realms of literature and into the low-culture and pop-culture world of blog posts, TV shows, and record collections. Which is, in and of itself, no bad thing. The true test of any radical theory or practice is whether it stays confined to the movement in which it originated—whether it's solely adopted by initiates and die-hards, or leaks out and permeates the way the norms and squares interact with the world. If it stays cool, it's not working. If it's working, it's probably not cool.

I, for example, cultivated most of my love for female confessional writing through the highly unserious and very norm-friendly medium of MTV. In 1993, when I was eleven years old, Liz Phair released *Exile in Guyville*: "I bet you fall in bed too easily with the beautiful girls who are shyly brave," was its opening line, and it got more parental-advisory-worthy from there, alternating rage with fuck-and-runs, "I want to be your blow-job queen" with "I'm a real cunt in spring." A year earlier, Tori Amos had released the self-described "diary" *Little Earthquakes*, delivering urgent first-person tales of religious repression, self-doubt, sexual violence, and boys who "said 'you're really an ugly girl, but I like the way you play.'" She'd name-check her menstrual cycle, describe her rape in wrenching detail, or just cry about her dad for five minutes, and it was all available in the resolutely apolitical aisles of Best Buy for only $9.99. She named Plath as a primary influence on her writing.

The list goes on—Fiona Apple's frank accounts of emotional damage and sexual violence; PJ Harvey reinventing "crazy ex-girlfriend" as a triumphant body-horror giantess on *Rid of Me*; even Courtney, bless her, was opening up—but the point is, I was raised on a rich slurry of gooey, bloody, painful, hysterical girl stuff. Nor did I ever learn to regard said stuff as shameful; when you're eleven years old, the coolest things are the ones famous rock stars do, so if famous rock stars were doing feminist first-person about sex and mental health, that was just what I liked. Of course, there was the not inconsiderable drawback that it was all market-researched and put on sale—I bought my feminist politics with my allowance, rather than joining an activist group for free—but that also made it widely available, and put the feminist first-person on offer to those without social connections to the movement. At the time, it felt immediate. It felt like community, even if I never knew the other women involved.

Community did enter into it, eventually. By the '00s, the female first-person was the province of the ladyblogs. Under the editorial guidance of Anna Holmes, *Jezebel* ran election coverage next to stories about getting a tampon lost up your vagina. *xoJane*, another feminist-leaning media outlet, has a section entitled, simply enough, "It Happened to Me." Sample articles include "It Happened to Me: I Let an Old Rich White Man Bankroll My Life . . . Even Though He Was Racist"; "I'm Being Stalked and Terrorized Because of My

Fat Acceptance Movie"; "I Was Suspended from My Teaching Job for Being Transgender." The political import is in the content, but the authority derives from the willingness to say *I, my, me.*

It's worth noting that both *xoJane* and *Jezebel* came under fire, upon their creation, for being the wrong kind of feminist, due in part to that use of the *I*: *Jezebel*'s posts about drinking and drug use were called "irresponsible," and their willingness to incorporate stories about dating or fashion next to stories about sexism and racism got them labeled fluffy. And it's true that the political usefulness or cultural relevance of the *xoJane I*—"It Happened to Me: A Gynecologist Found a Ball of Cat Hair in My Vagina," ran one infamous 2015 essay—could be, uh, fluid. Their original tagline, "a place where women go to be selfish, and where their selfishness is applauded," came in for a particularly harsh round of mocking. Soon enough, it was rewritten into "where women go to be their unabashed selves." But the same basic problem still applied: In a sexist context, and in the history of female silence, "unabashed selves" sounds synonymous with "selfish," or self-absorbed, or just plain contrary to the strong and self-sacrificing attitude many people assume a feminist is meant to have.

In the mid-twentieth century, confessing to an abortion or an affair with another woman would have been no less shocking than, say, *xoJane* writer Cat Marnell's notorious admission that she sometimes used Plan B as birth control. In fact, the shocking nature of those confessions was probably why there were rules about not yelling at the other women in the group. But in the commodified, hypercompetitive and (let us not forget) globally visible world of online media, firm rules about how to respond to a woman's story cannot possibly be created, let alone applied. And when a woman shocks us, it's easy to fault her story for not fitting into a pre-scribed and virtuous narrative of feminist womanhood. It's still all too tempting to evaluate a woman based on whether or not she is a "nice girl."

And then, there's the audience. The promise of consciousness-raising groups—community; a place to speak safely and freely, and to be heard—is both offered, and, in some ways, utterly denied in the new online world. There was a time, not long ago, when it was common to claim that blog comment sections were the consciousness-raising groups of the twenty-first century. I know women who forged deep and lasting friendships in the comments of *Jezebel*. But, though those gathering places fostered connection and understanding, they too wound up feeding the Internet's eternal need for quick-burning scandal.

In 2014, a woman left a comment on *xoJane* implying that she had been raped by Bright Eyes singer Conor Oberst. The comment—which she'd left under her real name—was publicized across the Internet, as was the content of her social-media presence, which was picked through for inconsistencies and signs of mental illness. Oberst himself sued her for libel. The woman retracted her claim. It's less a story about "false rape allegations" than it is about the trouble with building a community in a glass house: No matter what a woman said in her consciousness-raising group, she could say it without fear that she'd see it in tomorrow's headlines.

And so we're back to self-defense. As if we could ever really get away from it. "Something in Common" didn't really help Houston, in the long run. It read like defense, or denial, rather than romance. And the nation's eyes stayed on her marriage to Brown—often, eyes aided and abetted by reality-TV cameras—until it did, in fact, implode.

As for Britney—the boldest girl in a trainwreck year, the girl who had no defense but offense—she was the easiest player of all to knock out of the ring. When *Blackout* was released, on October 25, 2007, no one was talking about the music, or the lyrics. They were talking about the preview: A performance at the VMAs two months earlier, on September 9. Spears had refused to wear most of her costume at the last second, going out in a bra and panties. She'd stumbled a bit, been slow with her dance moves, apparently had trouble keeping up with her lip-sync.

In retrospect, it seems merely lackluster, a phoned-in performance by a visibly exhausted woman. In 2007, it was national news, and a potentially career-ending disgrace. It overshadowed *Blackout*'s release, overshadowed its lyrics, overshadowed Britney's statements—overshadowed everything, in fact, until she was taken to a psych ward in December, and finally gave us something worse to say. After that, what Britney Spears had to say about her own portrayal in the media counted for very little. She could talk. But who would listen to her? Who would believe some insane girl?

We do live in an unprecedented age of women's speech. Once again, social progress was matched by technological progress: As we pushed through the end of the twentieth century, and into the twenty-first, we got social media and smartphones. Surveillance went up again (nearly everyone you see is carrying a fully functional tape recorder, video camera, and publishing platform) but so did the ability to broadcast. It's not only common for women to leave public records of their lives, it's almost mandatory: Facebook, Tumblr, Twitter, and LinkedIn are all essential parts of having a social or professional life. The lesson of the twentieth century holds: As people become more visible, women become more visible. And this is especially true now that everyone, whether they realize it or not, is in the process of writing their memoirs.

So if speech were itself a cure for oppression, we would be living in a utopia. But it isn't, and we're not. Speech can do a lot of things—uncover a problem, refute a false narrative, provide a means of self-definition, leave a legacy—but the one thing it cannot do is shut up anyone else. No matter what you say, people will still be able to say whatever they like against you; the question is who people will believe. And, historically, in a clash of personal and cultural narratives, the winner is not likely to be female.

A two-hundred-year-old problem can't be ended with a slightly different mode of transmission. As long as the basic, underlying assumptions of what women "ought" to be remain the same, and as long as punishing "bad" women is acceptable, all of this marvelous technology will still only provide us with new ways to make women look like assholes. We can do it to ourselves now (oh, how I wish there was some kind of breathalyzer test I had to pass before I could use Twitter) but we can't stop doing it. Or at least, we haven't yet.

The journey from silence to speech—and from powerlessness to power, from unchallenged patriarchy to gender equality, because these are just different names for the same long road—is only halfway complete. We can tell the world who we are. But the world still doesn't have to listen. As long as the trainwreck industry keeps on rolling, all this liberating speech will tend to devolve into women trying to shout over or past their attackers.

The answer isn't to shut up. And the answer isn't simply to speak up individually and separately. It's to use our speech, while we have it, to ask why we keep doing this to each other—and to change what it means, not only to be a "bad" woman, but to be a woman at all. It's to keep asking the old, hard questions:

What is a nice girl?
Were you a nice girl?
Was anyone?
Who?
And for how long?

Part III

THE TRAINWRECK: HER ROLE

7

SCAPEGOAT

Every page of this book—of any book or story about celebrity trainwrecks—is haunted by Britney Spears. She hovers over every page, always looking to insert herself in there somewhere, always seeming like the right person to mention. It's impossible to think about trainwrecks for more than three consecutive seconds without landing on Britney: The Great Wreck, a woman whose suffering was, for the first decade of the 2000s, unavoidable. Every unflattering detail of her weight, her sex life, her mental health, her family discord, was broadcast twenty-four hours a day. We know almost every awful thing that has happened to Britney Spears since this glorious century began, and we usually don't know it because Britney Spears chose to disclose that information.

Though some part of this may simply be a matter of perspective—the Brits, for example, found their own Great Wreck in Amy Winehouse, or possibly Diana—Britney

Spears was, at the very least, the end of American pop-star mystique. There was more public information about her life, provided through more channels, than there had been for any other celebrity in history. She was the great test case for the hyper-invasive, rule-free, often amateur-run celebrity-gossip blogs which began their ascendance almost exactly when she did, in the early 2000s; she was the first great star whose narrative was defined as much by *TMZ* and *Perez Hilton* as it was by MTV or CNN.

The mainstream press, though bound by journalistic ethics in a way that Internet outlets were not, followed the blogs' lead. In 2008, the *Associated Press* released an internal memo instructing staffers that "now and for the foreseeable future, virtually everything involving Britney is a big deal." And that did mean *everything*: going to gas stations, eating a bag of Cheetos, walking her dog. But Britney's dedicated press corps was usually hoping for worse than that; her "shocking" downfall was a large and extremely profitable industry, wherein, as one anonymous photographer wrote for *Defamer* in 2013, "one shot of Britney slowly spiraling into insanity, one video of her shaving her head, or, the just one clip of her going fucking umbrella-attack crazy, could be your mortgage payment for the next year or a new car."

And yet, for all that, it's still hard to say exactly what Britney Spears did wrong. Mainly because Britney Spears did *everything* wrong, all at once. Certainly, sex was part of it. The fact that she'd lost her virginity to her live-in boyfriend was a national scandal; that he claimed she'd cheated on him was worse; photos of her crotch circulated through the tabloids as quickly as the kiss-and-tell confessions from her various unsuitable and scuzzy boyfriends, marking her irrevocably as a dirty girl, a contaminated and freakishly available female body. But Britney was also said to be ugly, undateable. She had children, gained weight, wore sweat-pants, had break-outs, not that this prevented literally any-one from looking up her naked body online. And Britney was a crazy ex-girlfriend—she was supposedly never the same after Justin Timberlake left her, supposedly descended into madness largely as the result of her divorce from Kevin Federline—or maybe just a crazy girl, a "habitual, frequent and continuous drug user" deemed legally unfit to raise her children, a madwoman who sometimes believed that her cell phone charger was taping her thoughts. Britney is an event horizon: Sex and mental illness and rejection and even death are drawn in and devoured, turned into one churning, ines-capable mass, by the One True Wreck, the all-consuming, monolithic spectacle of impermissible womanhood that was Britney.

So, at a certain point, analyzing the trainwrecks for what they *do* is not enough. You also have to ask why we need them—how a twenty-four-year-old woman's weight gain, or divorce, or occasional street-barf after a night of drink-ing, can possibly come to be such a massively profitable and popular source of entertainment, and what it is that we gain from collecting all these stories of female suffering. This is true, particularly, if we are women ourselves. And let's be clear: The primary audience for celebrity blogs, tabloids, and reality TV shows is not straight men. Women are the ones who buy these stories. We're the ones who enjoy them. We're the ones these narratives are shaped for and aimed at. We're the reason they exist. But what is it, exactly, that we're enjoying?

To begin to answer that question, it's worthwhile to go back, to a time before Crazy Britney. To ask ourselves, not how she "fell," but what she fell from, and not how "bad" she was, but what exactly we meant when we called her "good."

"Britney Spears extends a honeyed thigh across the length of the sofa." Thus begins the April 1999 *Rolling Stone* cover story about Britney Spears, published when she was seventeen years old.

Britney was a role model, that year. She prayed every night on her tour bus, because she couldn't get to church often enough; she dealt with stress by writing in her prayer journal. She was a virgin, and she intended to stay that way until marriage, because sex was sacred. In the *Rolling Stone* piece, she told reporter Steven Daly that she couldn't watch *South Park* because it was "sacrilegious," and couldn't drink anything other than the occasional glass of wine, supervised by her mother, because she didn't like to feel "out of control." She was a proud conservative, raised to believe that women ought to take pride in being homemakers; years later, at the height of the Iraq War, she would tell Tucker Carlson that Americans shouldn't question the president. In that first profile, the one from 1999, she said that she didn't understand why there had been such an uproar over the pigtails and Catholic schoolgirl outfits in the ". . . Baby One More Time" video—despite coming up with the idea, Britney was supposedly too sheltered to realize that they had been lifted directly from the iconography of "barely legal" porn, in which adult men fucked teenage girls—and her bedroom, Daly reported, was full of dolls.

"You want to be a good example for kids out there and not do something stupid. Kids have low self-esteem, and then the peer pressures come and they go into a wrong crowd. That's when all the bad stuff starts happening, drugs and stuff." That was how a typical Britney Spears quote ran, in 1999.

But, in between visits to Britney's bedroom, Steven Daly made sure to note her thighs and what she did with them. He made sure to include lines like "Spears' pink T-shirt is distended by her ample chest, and her silky white shorts—with dark blue piping—cling snugly to her hips." On the cover of the magazine (her first cover, shot by Dave LaChappelle) Britney was shown reclining in underpants and a bra, cradling a stuffed Teletubby doll. She was shot from above—

the same angle you'd have if you were the horny track coach or the well-endowed grown-up neighbor in one of those barely legal fantasies, descending onto her prone body— and her crumpled satin bedding called to mind the satin Marilyn Monroe had lain on in her own famously leaked nudes. Inside the magazine, you could find her posing in a cheerleader outfit, coyly pulling the skirt up toward her hips, or posing in that doll-stuffed bedroom in underwear and high heels, or shot from behind, walking a pink tricycle, wearing short-shorts with the word "BABY" emblazoned in rhinestones on one ass-cheek. Men were supposed to want to sleep with Britney, that was clear enough. But they were supposed to want it specifically because she was a child.

I was also seventeen, the year that *Rolling Stone* cover came out. I had a subscription. And, on the basis of that story, and the ". . . Baby One More Time" video, I truly believed that I hated Britney Spears.

I was just starting to get catcalled on the street, that year; I already knew at least two girls who'd been raped when they passed out at parties. At twelve, I'd given my phone number to a grown-up over AIM and gotten heavy-breathing phone calls; at sixteen, I had been asked to kiss a twenty-something man's girlfriend on a "dare," and I was still trying to figure out how I felt about the look on his face when I followed through. I was also used to the more routine indignities— being groped, being leered at, being flashed—though that didn't make them any less awful. Britney and I were both virgins, and like Britney, I told people that I intended to stay that way until I was married, but in my case, it was less about virtue than terror: Every experience I'd had of sex, or of men's desire for sex, had been hostile and unwanted. I didn't plan to "save" my virginity for my husband because I wanted to please Jesus, but because I was scared of being naked and alone in the presence of someone who didn't love me. The last thing I was prepared to deal with, that year, was the idea that grown-ups could find my reticence and inexperience *sexy*; at seventeen, I didn't want any adult men thinking about my chest size, let alone my potentially honeyed thighs.

Yet, somehow, I didn't blame the guys themselves. The person I blamed and hated was Britney, the girl who stoked their appetite; the girl who was my age, tasked with representing girls my age to the world, and who let men think we liked the attention. Somehow, in my heart of hearts, I believed that if Britney Spears were not famous, I could walk down the street without hearing a single catcall. Without Britney, other girls would be safe.

It never occurred to me to wonder whether Britney herself liked the attention. I never stopped to think that she might have been frightened, too: that being asked to pose in your underwear, by a group of adults, might be just as strange as being asked to kiss some grown man's girlfriend, or that having your breasts lovingly described for an audience of thousands might be far more invasive than hearing a few words thrown from a moving car. I didn't read the interview she gave *Rolling Stone* in 2000, in which she worried about the number of grown men in her audience, and described being attacked by one of them: "This guy jumps up on the stage, takes his shirt off and comes running. I think the crowd thought it was supposed to happen, but security jumped on the stage and got him off." Later, in the same interview, she told the reporter that "I don't want to be part of someone's *Lolita* thing. It kind of freaks me out." For that matter, despite the fact that I hate-read the first *Rolling Stone* profile at least three or four times, I somehow managed to miss the part where Daly mentioned that Britney was being routinely assaulted: "Alone in the house one night, she hid from a prowler lurking at the window; her mother surprised another as he was hailing to her through a locked bedroom window." I was so unhappy, and so afraid, that I never thought about whether Britney Spears was safe or happy, nor did I consider any of the plentiful evidence that she was not.

Worrying about Britney would have required seeing her as a real girl my own age, capable of experiencing the same trauma, subject to the same pressures. And I couldn't do that: In my mind, she was an icon, a symbol, a teenager-shaped screen onto which I could project all my own frustration with how I was expected to behave, or how men saw me. And, moreover, I managed to convince myself that seeing her in that light—as an object, a problem rather than a person—was an act of feminism. I didn't hate Britney Spears. I hated being a seventeen-year-old girl. But, because she was a seventeen-year-old girl herself, and visible, she was an ideal scapegoat; she was someone I could punish for the crime of being female.

Which is to say: We rarely love or hate public figures for who they are. We can't; we don't know them. At a certain point, the media narrative surrounding celebrities stops being about the specifics of their lives or personalities and enters the realm of myth. Stars are only stars because they represent something larger than themselves, some archetype, or a story we enjoy telling. From the moment Britney became a pop star, "Britney Spears" rather than "Britney from *The Mickey Mouse Club*" or "that cute little girl on *Star Search*," she was burdened with the weight of representation, made to mean something more or other than herself. She was the "Queen of Teen," the face of what we expected from young girls in America, and she reflected back those expectations faithfully, with all their inherent problems and contradictions kept intact. Britney was only, ever, what all girls should be, even if it didn't make sense for one girl to be all those things, and even if asking girls to be all those things would hurt them.

Trainwrecks, as public figures, are necessarily also myths. But they're the villains of the story; they're our mon-

sters and demons, images of what we fear, and who we fear
becoming. I hated Britney early on, because I hated being
forced into the role she seemingly enjoyed playing; I wanted
to reject the feminine ideal she supposedly embodied, and
I wound up rejecting *her*. But every wreck is a potential role
that women need or want to reject; the magnitude of our hatred for them is determined by how powerfully we fear what
they represent. In Britney's case, she represented the end of
youth, and the corruption of purity: She was the pretty, good
little girl who became ugly and bad when she grew up, the
"Queen of Teen" who was used-up and over-the-hill by age
twenty-five. She was the Wages of Feminism, the working
mother who tried to have it all and wound up nearly dropping her baby onto the sidewalk. She was the cost of public
life, for women. (A common moral: Kylie Jenner is the latest
to be DESTROYED BY FAME, according to my supermarket
check-out counter. Apparently, this entails COCAINE, MORE
SECRET SURGERY, & SEX WITH HER BOYFRIEND'S ENEMY,
though some time later it also entailed a clip of Jenner running into the magazine cover at a drug store, and collapsing
into mortified laughter). Or, she was the price of thinking
for oneself, as a woman whose attempts at adult indepen-
dence had (supposedly) driven her insane.

But the tale of the Virgin Queen dethroned is a story
with tremendous resonance, in a culture that loves youth
and hates women. It's powerful, especially, for women, who
are taught to fear and delay their own aging process from

the moment they hit puberty. Just as I was able to project all of my own fears and insecurities onto the image of the virginal-but-hot teenage girl, adult women had a tremendous amount of culturally instilled self-loathing to bestow upon grown-up, washed-out Britney: Whether as a too-perfect girl or an imperfect woman, a vehicle for the anxieties of adolescence or the self-loathing of adulthood, she got it from both ends, a target for every age-based insecurity any given woman could summon up.

In fact, that particular story of virgin sacrifice is so salable that we've kept finding new people about whom to tell it, changing very few details in the retelling. In the late 2000s, just as Britney's "meltdown" was reaching its peak, we created a new teenage dream, a kid named Miley. She, too was a Disney Channel alum, who made her name playing the wildly popular Hannah Montana. (All-American girl by day, pop star by night!) She, too, was Southern, conservative, possessed of plentiful aw-shucks charm, a self-declared virgin—in fact, she upped the ante by wearing a purity ring, signifying that she'd sworn before God not to have premarital sex—but still, maddeningly, sexual. She had a course to run. And she ran it, in Britney's footsteps.

Miley's "downfall"—her transformation into the tongue-wagging, joint-toking, Robin-Thicke-"molesting" outrage factory we covered in the first chapter—was practically planned from the start of her career. After years of rehearsing the narrative (not just Britney, but Lindsay Lohan,

Amanda Bynes, Winona Ryder, Drew Barrymore; one early iteration featured Judy Garland) it can now be executed with the relentless professionalism of a Broadway musical. For example, in order to accomplish the 2013 image reboot that saved her flagging album sales—the image reboot that resulted in her album *Bangerz* and the birth of the Miley we know—Cyrus hired a new manager, Larry Rudolph. He's best known as the man who launched the career of Britney Spears. Miley Cyrus still doesn't have any drug convictions, DUIs, institutionalizations, high-profile firings, or, really, any of the misfortunes we associate with the story; in a way, her train never wrecked at all. She might as well have hired Michael Bay and Industrial Light & Magic to create an incredibly realistic scene of a train derailing, so that she could walk away in slow motion, coolly donning sunglasses, as it exploded.

Celebrities' lives are their own, and individual, but their stories are not: They're manufactured by entertainment and media professionals who know how to hone a narrative for maximum impact, people who are hired specifically for their skill at creating marketable personas out of mere people, or transforming data and detail into character and plot. Stars and publicists can and do cooperate in the construction of plot points, by providing stories under cover of anonymity—if you see "a friend" cited, it may well be the celebrity's PR wing, trying to keep their client visible between projects; when Kim Kardashian worked for Paris Hilton, one of her jobs was providing stories to *InTouch Magazine*—or permitting the publication of a less embarrassing story to avoid the publication of a more embarrassing one. (Harvey Levin of *TMZ* reportedly keeps a "vault" of damaging information; if the target wants to keep something in "the vault," and unseen by the public, he or she needs to provide Levin with a better story.) Once the raw data has been obtained, it is then finessed by people with an eye for drama; the editor in chief of *InTouch* came to the magazine from *Soap Opera Update*, and, according to a profile by Anne Helen Petersen, "former employees remember [him] laying out a four-act cover drama for what would happen between Brad Pitt and Angelina Jolie at the beginning of each month—a pregnancy, for example, followed by a breakup scare, a reconciliation, and then marriage rumors."

Trainwrecks are a business. Specifically, an entertainment business. They come to you through people who live and die by how many eyeballs and mouse-clicks they (we) can collect, and who therefore learn to shape even the most gnarled and unruly of biographies into something with the clean, salable power of a familiar story. The trainwrecks, like everyone else, are written in the way that will best connect with the widest number of people at any given time. So they are not only a chance to see our familiar female monsters embodied and serialized—the Slut, the Clingy Ex, the Aging Beauty—but a peephole into the dark undercurrents of the culture at large, the secret fears and lurking menaces of their moment.

For example, in April 1999, at the precise moment that Britney Spears arrived in the public consciousness, the country was tearing itself apart over the question of women, and age, and sex. And this particular wreck wasn't confined to pop radio and magazine covers; it was happening in the halls of Congress, and concerned the highest office in the world.

•

Anatomy of a Trainwreck

HILLARY RODHAM CLINTON & MONICA LEWINSKY

It was not surprising, in 1998, to suggest that President Bill Clinton probably had affairs. Most people assumed he did; if they were smart, they assumed that men in politics, generally, had them. Kennedy had Marilyn; Earl Long had Blaze Starr; the speaker of the House, Newt Gingrich, had left his first wife in the middle of her cancer treatment so that he could marry his mistress. Nelson Rockefeller had served as the vice president of the United States, and had gone on from there to be the governor of New York, and had gone on from *there* to die while having sex with his twenty-five-year-old assistant. When it came to Clinton, there was too much in the way of precedent, and far too many rumors, for the possibility to be entirely disregarded.

And besides, there was his wife. That year, it seemed there was no one—liberal or conservative, male or female— who entirely liked or trusted Hillary Clinton. She was a practicing lawyer, where no other first lady had pursued a postgraduate degree. She kept an office in the West Wing, helped make staffing decisions, and pushed for universal healthcare, where other first ladies had been decorative and far removed from the center of power. When people suggested Hillary might take a more traditional wifely role, she was openly disgusted: In her first *60 Minutes* interview, she rolled her eyes imagining herself as "some little woman, standing by my man, like Tammy Wynette," and scoffed at the idea that she could have "stayed home and baked cookies and had teas," rather than litigating cases. The *New York Post* called her "a buffoon, an insult to most women"; there was an episode of *Nightline* devoted to parsing the "cookies" comment. (OMINOUS VOICE-OVER: "The damage had been done. She'd been tagged an elitist and an ultra-feminist.") Conservative men loathed her for being a man-hating feminazi, women loathed her for calling them "little," and both groups loathed her degree of influence over the administration, an attitude that could be neatly summed up by one oddly prescient joke during the '92 campaign:

"Then, there's Clinton," incumbent George Bush Sr. said. "A very formidable candidate. But would Mario Cuomo run as Hillary's vice president?"

The jokes kept coming. Throughout the early '90s, novelty shops sold "Billary" T-shirts and mugs, decorated with cartoons of Bill and Hillary merged into a freakish con-joined president. Hillary's lust for power, the joke went, was so overwhelming that she'd actually inserted herself into her husband's skin—erasing the distinction between their dif-ferent bodies, their different jobs, their different genders—in order to more effectively control him.

But that, according to the common wisdom, was about the only kind of lustful insertion you were likely to see in the Clinton marriage. They did not, reportedly, love each other, or even like each other; they were co-workers who'd made a marriage of convenience, or else a contemporary version of Lady Macbeth and her weak-willed husband, an unsexed and dangerous woman pushing her man onto the national stage for the sake of her own ambitions. In pri-vate, Hillary was said to be a shrew, a violent and unlov-able nightmare. Shortly after Bill Clinton's inauguration, the *Chicago Sun-Times* alleged that she had broken a lamp during an argument, a story that quickly ballooned out—without verification or sourcing—into a tale about how she had *thrown* the lamp at him, which then turned into a story about how she'd thrown multiple objects, including a Bible, which, before long, was a story about the president and first lady punching each other. (In one particularly delightful variant, after the five-foot-five Hillary started a fistfight with her six-foot-two husband and desecrated the Holy Bible by us-ing it as a weapon, she then "lit up a cigarette to punish her smoke-allergic husband." So . . . I guess she won?) Despite the fact that they had a daughter, no one really believed they had sex; Hillary, at least, was usually presumed not to want or enjoy it. When the rumor mill did allow her some kind of desire, it was always perverse or annihilating. One popular rumor was that Hillary was a closeted lesbian, who tolerated Bill's girlfriends because she was busy with her own; according to another, she'd had an affair with Vince Foster, and had him killed to cover it up.

So—the thinking went—of course Bill Clinton had affairs. What else was the man going to do? Have sex with Hillary? Still, when the details of one such affair were revealed to the public, they were enough to send the news media, and the public, spinning out into a year-long paroxysm of horror, disillusionment, and disgust. They also mandated the creation of a new villain in the narrative: Rather than sticking Hillary with the blame for every real or perceived problem with the Clinton administration, we began assigning it to the Other Woman.

You know. *That* Woman.

Monica Lewinsky had been twenty-one years old, and a White House intern, when she first met the president. What they did, when they met, was covered in exhaustive and pornographic detail by *The Starr Report*, prosecutor Ken Starr's investigation of their relationship, supposedly undertaken because the president had denied that relationship under oath. Clinton defended himself by claiming that he'd been

asked about "sexual relations," which had been legally defined as touching the genitals of another person for sexual gratification, and that—as the recipient of oral sex—he
hadn't, strictly speaking, touched Lewinsky's. In the immortal words of *The Starr Report*, he argued that "she engaged in sexual relations but he did not." (Think about *that*
the next time your partner won't return the favor.) But this
maneuver only made things worse: Lewinsky was seized,
threatened with twenty-seven years in prison, and interrogated until she gave up specific, humiliating details on
each and every way Bill Clinton had ever come into contact
with her body. Who touched what, *with* what, who came,
when they came, what they said about it, or felt about it, and
how often phone sex came into the equation. Soon enough,
it was all out there, a matter of public record, reprinted
in *The Washington Post* and as a hard-cover book available in
Wal-Mart.

But when people read *The Starr Report*, it wasn't merely
the salacious details—the thong-flashing, the blow-job-
giving, the cigar going where no cigar had gone before—
that sparked their outrage. It was *her*: Monica, the girl whose
voice permeated every page. *The Starr Report* was, among
other things, an excruciatingly detailed first-person account
of how Monica Lewinsky had endured a bad breakup. And
her worst crime was not lying, or even having sex with a
powerful man; it was that she fell in love with him, and refused to let go of the relationship when he wanted it to end.

The affair hit the rocks when Monica was dismissed from the White House and moved to the Pentagon. Her superiors had noticed how much time she spent alone with the president, and thought (not unreasonably, as it turned out) that rumors of an affair could create trouble for the administration. Monica was "devastated," not only because sexual harassment laws had been created to prevent women from losing their jobs if they were thought to pose a sexual temptation to their bosses, but because she thought, "I was never going to see the president again." In the months after her transfer, Clinton did in fact phase her out of his life, and eventually dumped her outright, something she dealt with by trying—over and over again—to see him in person, to get close again, to change his mind.

Though it was the Clinton camp's decision to spread the tale that Monica was a "stalker," a delusional and predatory woman who'd fantasized a relationship with the president, it was the work of Starr and his allies to turn Monica's lovesick humiliation into news. The report made sure to note that Clinton's secretary, Betty Currie, called her a "pain in the neck" and complained about the "many phone calls" in which Monica was "distraught and sometimes in tears over her inability to get in touch with the president." Vernon Jordan, who'd been tasked with finding her another job, was quoted calling Monica a "highly emotional lady." We got to read copious snippets from Monica's unsent letters, which ran the full range of embarrassing post-breakup emotions, from irate to abject and back again: "Any normal person would have walked away from this and said, 'He doesn't call me, he doesn't want to see me—screw it. It doesn't matter.' I can't let go of you," ran one such note. By the time the year was up, we would hear a tape of Monica sobbing to Linda Tripp, who was, unbeknownst to her, taping their phone calls on the advice of her literary agent. Monica's voice was so mangled with snot and pain that you could hardly make out the words: *I can't take it, I can't **take** it any more.*

Where Hillary was presumed to be cold and emotionless, Monica was *all* emotion, a throbbing mess of tears and needs. Where Hillary was seen as purely political, happy to accept a loveless marriage if it helped her make national policy, Monica returned to "love," over and over again, as her justification, even when it made her seem clueless about the political context: In her interview with Barbara Walters, given in March 1999, while Clinton was facing impeachment, Monica called him her "soulmate." Where Hillary was perceived as being sexless, Monica was all sex, a "blowjob queen" whose proclivities and underwear preferences were smeared all over every newspaper, magazine, and late-night talk-show monologue in the nation. And where Hillary was presumed to be calculating, all brain and no heart, Monica could seem, at times, crushingly naive—not stupid, precisely, but not tremendously rational, either, led by her heart to the exclusion of even basic common sense. Long after the relationship ended, when he'd been avoiding her for months, and just after a screaming fight in which she threatened to tell her parents about the affair and he said he wished he'd never gotten involved with her, Bill Clinton made a joke about maybe being single one day. She chose to interpret all this as a sign that he wanted to leave his wife for her: "I just knew he was in love with me," she said.

These women had nothing in common. Well, one thing: They were both blamed for Bill Clinton's cheating. In her 2014 *Vanity Fair* essay about how the scandal had ruined her life, Monica made sure to remind her readers of an *Observer* round-table (NEW YORK SUPERGALS LOVE THAT NAUGHTY PREZ) in which various women writers discussed the affair. She mentioned her pain at hearing herself described as "not pretty" and "not brilliant" ("My first job out of college was at the White House," she noted), and her horror when it was suggested that she could "rent out her mouth." What Lewinsky did not mention was what those same women said about Hillary Clinton.

She was unattractive, first of all. "Isn't it interesting that Bill doesn't go for women that look like Hillary?" Francine Prose noted. Patricia Marx tut-tutted the fact that "Hillary Clinton changed her hairstyle one million times, and the one way she didn't try was the one way that works." All were agreed that Hillary was probably not loving or vulnerable enough to be truly hurt by the affair: "I think [Hillary] would actually be more effective if she showed a little weakness," Katie Roiphe said. "There's something a little

steely, and people are suspicious because she seems very political." As always, Hillary was all brain and ambition, without bodily desire or human emotion: Erica Jong advanced
the idea that "she has so much power over his mind that
she almost doesn't care who has power temporarily over
his cock."

Hillary Clinton and Monica Lewinsky, predictably, disliked each other. Hillary privately told her friend Diane Blair
that Monica was a "narcissistic Loony-Toon," which became
public when Blair's papers were published after her death. A
few months later, Monica objected to the fact that "Hillary
Clinton wanted it on record that she was lashing out at her
husband's mistress." In other words, Hillary called Monica
crazy and Monica called Hillary calculating, each woman
throwing the other's existing media narrative back into her
face. Yet they were also mirror images of each other. They
were the Betty and Veronica of sexism: The icy blonde and
the overheated brunette, the prude and the slut, the shrew-
ish wife and the trashy mistress, the sexless middle-aged
woman and the trampy young one, the frigid, man-hating
intellectual and the needy, man-hungry ditz.

But neither woman was acceptable. Neither woman was
deemed worthy of love, or even of being liked. While their
media narratives were crafted to portray them as opposites
in every respect, neither of the two models of womanhood
they represented courted anything but scorn, disdain, or
vilification. Trainwrecks are, often, photo negatives of ac-

ceptable femininity—the opposite of what a woman is meant to be—but, when you turned Hillary inside out, you got Monica, and when you turned Monica the other way around, Hillary emerged. No matter which side of the coin you found your own face on, you were a wreck. There was no way to win the game; no "good" woman left to be.

Well: There was, potentially, *one* good woman. But finding her would be nearly impossible. She would have to be young, to avoid the stigma of '70s feminism and middle-aged unfuckability that had tarred Hillary. But she couldn't be "young" in the way that Monica was, which had involved adventure and experimentation; her youth would have to be clear of youthful folly. She'd have to be hot, and comfortable with getting men hot—she couldn't be cold or frigid, like Hillary—but she couldn't actually have sex, as Monica had, because that would taint her with the stigma of sluttiness. The ideal woman would have to be innocent, in both the sexual and the legal sense of the word. She also couldn't be a stuck-up, ambitious intellectual, like Hillary; but, unlike Monica, she'd have to be sensible and morally upright enough to never make any bad decisions. And she'd have to be conservative, to avoid the stigma and scandal of the Clinton administration; yet, for all that, she couldn't be prudish or uncool about her conservatism, like actual Republicans, because she would have to avoid the backlash facing them, too.

To save herself from the hatred that defined the public lives of Hillary Clinton and Monica Lewinsky, the ideal woman would have to steer between them, like Scylla and Charybdis, navigating the currents without being swept toward either side: Virgin and pin-up, wide-eyed innocent and worldly temptress, icon of cool and conservative Christian role model, she would always have to be both and neither, everything and nothing, and she would have to be able to do all of this when she was still very, very young.

One month after March 1999, when Monica Lewinsky gave her Barbara Walters interview, *Rolling Stone* ran the first-ever magazine cover featuring Britney Spears.

•

Britney didn't happen by accident. She was what we needed; the answer to a question no one wanted to admit asking. But then, all of the women discussed in this book emerged into the public eye, and became a central and charged topic of conversation, precisely because they embodied the anxieties of their time.

Jane Eyre, for example, frightened people, not only because it was sexy, or because of the suspicion that it was written by a woman, but because the narrator was a governess; it shocked middle-class and wealthy readers with the uncomfortable awareness that *servants*, the non-persons they invited into their homes and interacted with all day, could also be sexually available women, capable of forming their own affections and ambitions. Valerie Solanas and

Sylvia Plath were the uncomfortable spectres of feminism's second wave: the crazy, man-slaughtering lesbian and the bitterly vengeful, bile-spilling housewife, given voice, and hence, giving reality to the idea that women might hit back. Billie Holiday was a black woman, a queer woman, a survivor, and an addict, thrown into a culture that was hospitable to none of those identities; Mary Wollstonecraft was a single mother in an era when single motherhood was a tragedy tantamount to death, and a French sympathizer at the moment when the French Revolution and democracy as a concept terrified all of Europe; Harriet Jacobs was, most obviously of all, a freed slave. Each woman was frightening, not just because of who she was, but because of what she was. Each woman had to walk through the world as the embodiment of an era's fears.

As the centuries move forward, the anxieties change with the terrain. Whitney Houston, one of the first black women to be treated like a mainstream "pop princess," was a symbol for black women's upward mobility; she was turned by reality TV and hostile media coverage into a woman that *The O'Reilly Factor* called "just another crackhead," a loud, scary, down-market stereotype. You could even make a case for Hillary and Monica themselves as the scapegoats for second- and third-wave feminism, respectively: The second wave told women to work for equality and advance in the workplace, which Hillary did, and was hated for doing, and the third told women to embrace their sexuality and see femininity as a source of power, which Monica did, and was hated for doing.

Britney was the most spectacular implosion of all, the place where it all fell apart. She was the perfect girl, who fractured and shattered in agonizing slow motion, to show us that even female perfection—even nearly *impossible* perfection, the contradictory not-this-nor-that, both-this-*and*-that tightrope Britney was made to walk—was a fault line, a disaster waiting to happen. After two centuries of feminist progress and increasing female agency, the journey that started with Mary Wollstonecraft and seemed to proceed through to Hillary Clinton wound up with Britney: a reminder that no matter how rich, or important, or powerful she was, no matter how "good" or how beautiful she seemed, even the perfect girl would get drunk one day, or lose a boyfriend, or gain weight, or age, or get sad, or get sick. And when she did, we would be there. Ready and waiting to take her down.

And, since the wrecks exist to embody our private monsters, to absorb and reflect women's insecurities, it would seem to follow that the sheer fact of being women was also our most profound insecurity. Even if we got everything right, being female was a flaw that we could never quite correct or live down.

There may never be a spectacle to rival Britney's. Even contemporaries who actually died—Amy, Whitney, Anna Nicole Smith—seemed like dim echoes, unable to match her for sheer humiliation. And Britney, in the end, did not even die: She was buried alive. Put under her father's conservatorship, she now lives under a form of legal control that is normally reserved for late-stage Alzheimer's patients and people with severe developmental disabilities; she is no longer legally allowed to decide whether she gets married, or where she lives, or who her doctors will be, or how to spend her money. She can no longer legally sign a contract. She is not allowed to use her cell phone unless her father approves. It reads like a cruel joke: The "Queen of Teen," the ideal American girl-woman, is now condemned to be a child in the eyes of the law for, potentially, the rest of her life.

But, just as she was breaking down, something strange happened: The world began to love Britney Spears again. The endless, devouring need to see her fall apart and break down was replaced with something more like sisterhood, a desire to see her well, or happy, or free. Feminist writers began to attack and reject nasty or invasive press coverage, to protest the conservatorship that made her, in the words of Michelle Dean, "a prisoner"; in 2014, when *Medium* ran an article by Taffy Brodesser-Acker about her Las Vegas residency, Britney's central place in gender politics was so assured that Brodesser-Acker could confidently call her "a feminist role model for single working mothers here and everywhere" without fear of being laughed out of town.

Brodesser-Acker also quoted fans talking about the train-wreck years. Here was their assessment:

"Oh, I loved it," said a fan named Andrea. "She was just saying fuck you to the world over and over. This was who I knew she was. In the early 2000s, she was a phony. *This* was really her."

Meanwhile, mainstream pop-culture coverage stopped using words like "meltdown" and "white trash" and started calling Britney words like "icon," and "living legend." They referred to a woman in her early thirties as if she were the battle-scarred survivor of some ancient war, which—in a way—she was. Her suffering had purified her, allowed us to identify with her in a way that perfection had precluded. The ideal girl broke down, became a monster, and emerged on the other side as a real, flawed, and struggling woman, with plenty of reasons to say "fuck you" to the world. *That* woman, we didn't have to see as a role model. That woman, we could simply love.

And she wasn't the only one. After the Lewinsky scandal died down, and Bill Clinton's presidency ended, Hillary Clinton—the woman who spent most of the '90s being reviled for being "too political," too baldly interested in power—successfully ran for the Senate in New York.

And she ran for president. And she became secretary of state. And she ran for president again. By 2015, when people wondered who Hillary Clinton's vice-presidential pick would be, they weren't joking. They were also faced with the

odd fact that Hillary Clinton—elitist! Ultra-feminist! Enemy of boners everywhere!—was, by a substantial margin,
the "most admired woman anywhere in the world." The
one thing about her that reliably brought on the most vilification—a *woman*! Who was interested in *politics*! Why, she
acted as if *she* could be president!—turned out to be the one
thing she excelled at for the next several decades of her life.

It's not that people stopped hating Hillary Clinton, exactly. Plenty of people still hate her; people, particularly
men, always have, and they probably always will. Since
2005 alone, conservative writer Ed Klein has published
three straight books about how much he hates her, which
are most famous for the theory that Hillary Clinton is so
frigid that Chelsea Clinton had to be the product of marital
rape. During her first Presidential run, left-wing anchorman
Keith Olbermann publicly expressed a desire for "somebody who can take her into a room and only he comes out";
during her second, *Nation* editor Doug Henwood (author of
such subtle and nuanced works as "Stop Hillary!") posted
a Photoshopped image of her eating a baby. She still has a
remarkable ability to turn otherwise reasonable people into
tinfoil-hat-wearing conspiracy theorists.

But in all the fury, the conspiracy theorists and angry
men seemed to miss one of the strangest facts about Hillary Clinton: Gravity works differently on her. You can trip
her up or knock her over, but when Hillary falls, she falls
up. Every baby-eating Photoshop, every public humiliation,

every unflattering picture or crushing defeat or speculation as to her fuckability or "likability," has been the prequel to Hillary Clinton making another unprecedented step forward, doing one more thing no one thought she (or, for that matter, women) would ever be able to do. It is too early to know how history will regard Hillary Clinton. But history will certainly regard her—probably with no small amount of confusion—as a woman who appeared in the age of the "ambition gap," and who just threw a grappling hook over to the other side of the damn thing and swung across it like Tarzan.

Monica Lewinsky, at first glance, seems to have emerged as the sole loser. She had neither Britney's fame nor Hillary's base of power from which to rebuild; she spent her adult life trying in vain to hit on some viable form of employment (handbag designing, weight-loss campaign spokeswomanship), earning her masters' degree in social psychology, and being rejected from every job to which she applied. At forty, she is still trying to build a life from the wreckage of *The Starr Report.* But when she published the essay in *Vanity Fair* about her experience, denouncing the "culture of humiliation" that had done her in and driven her to the verge of suicide, young feminists were listening, and ready to back her up: Why *had* Maureen Dowd won a Pulitzer for comparing Monica to Glenn Close in *Fatal Attraction?* Why had the comments about her focused so often on her weight, on the blow jobs she'd given rather than the orgasms she'd had; why had calling her a "blow-job queen" or "Portly Pepperpot" ever been okay? Why had we all been so willing to buy the line of *The Starr Report* or the Clinton defenders, and see her as stupid, or a stalker, or a slut: Wasn't it possible that the three S's didn't apply, that she had just been a twenty-something girl with a misguided crush on a notoriously charming man, operating out of pure, foolish, human feeling?

Trainwrecks are myths, yes. They are our monsters: cultural monsters, who embody the tensions of our moment or our expectations of women, and deeply personal monsters, who embody the parts of ourselves we are most afraid of. But there is another thing to note about all this: We are all, each and every one of us, our own worst monsters. And we all yearn, despite this fact, to be loved.

The trainwreck is the inverse of what a woman ought to be: She is demanding, sexually voracious, where women are meant to be merely sexy, and receptive to outside desire. She is emotional, needy, where women are meant to be likable and agreeable at all times. Where women are meant to care for others—where Britney was slammed for not caring enough about her children, and Hillary was slammed for not caring enough about Bill, and Monica was slammed for not caring enough about Hillary—the trainwreck is utterly vulnerable, sometimes incapable of keeping even herself going, desperately in need of care.

But there is no one woman who is purely sexy, purely agreeable, purely caring; there is no one devoid of appetite, or sadness, or rage, or the need to be taken care of. There is no "ideal girl." We tried to manufacture her, at one point, and she turned out to be the biggest wreck of all.

There is an undeniable cruelty in our need for stories about wrecked women. We do sometimes seek them out for reasons of pure schadenfreude, or internalized misogyny. We can use them as projection screens for our own fears and failings, or look to them to confirm that we're doing our own gender correctly. It's understandable that we would: Women are punished, cruelly, for failing to be appropriately feminine, and there are dozens or hundreds of ways to get it wrong. Tuning into a reality-TV show where women punch each other while vying for the affections of some spray-tanned has-been, or looking at pictures of a celebrity stumbling drunkenly out of a car without her panties on, offers us a real if short-lived brand of comfort: It confirms that the standard for acceptable behavior is much lower than previously supposed, that if we haven't punched anyone, or fucked Bret Michaels, or forgotten to wear pants today, we are at least doing better than someone else. We can look to the trainwrecks in order to tell ourselves, *well, at least I'm not that girl.*

But even if we're not that girl, we're never perfect girls. And our love for messes—our willingness to accept and validate and admire even the most formerly polarizing of women, once we've seen enough of their suffering—suggests that there is a kinder and healthier reason to enjoy train-wreck stories. These women, with all their loudness and messiness, their public loneliness and weepy outbursts, their falling down and falling apart, are the image of our own vulnerable selves, the wild and agonized messes we all conceal beneath our hopefully acceptable personas. They can embody the women we hope not to be, but they can also give a public voice to our own suffering; they can be the women who speak for us, when they say "fuck you" to the world.

Women hate trainwrecks to the extent that we hate ourselves. We love them to the extent that we want our own flaws and failings to be loved. The question, then, is choosing between the two; whether we'll continue to demand that women in the public eye act as our personal scapegoats, for the crime of being human, or whether we'll go ahead and admit that—to quote a former president; I apologize in advance for this one—we feel their pain.

8

REVOLUTIONARY

If you are ever in the mood to feel grateful for modernity and all its conveniences, there are few things more apt to do the trick than a book entitled *Curious Punishments of Bygone Days*. Written in 1896 by colonial historian Alice Morse Earle, it is a compendium of all the tortures embraced, by our Revolutionary forefathers, as a means of correcting bad behavior. Public branding; holes poked through the tongue; ears lopped off as a special punishment for recidivism; I'm telling you, this club has *everything*. Most of it, as Earle notes, carried out in public to make it more emotionally painful.

Being a woman, Earle seems to have been particularly interested in which humiliations were doled out to women, and why. So, not only can you find historical evidence of our forefathers discovering the nation's first Paris Hilton ("Anne ux. Richard Walker being cast out of the church of Boston for intemperate drinking from one inn to another, and for light and wanton behavior, was the next day called before the governour and the treasurer, and convict by two witnesses, and was stripped naked one shoulder, and tied to the whipping-post, but her punishment was respited") or penning delightful poems in praise of waterboarding their wives to end an argument ("No brawling wives, no furious wenches / No fire so hot but water quenches"), you can also get several instructive glimpses of the actual women who were thus shamed. For example, this woman:

> *One of the latest, and certainly the most notorious sentences to ducking was that of Mrs. Anne Royall, of Washington, D.C., almost in our own day. This extraordinary woman had lived through an eventful career in love and adventure; she had been stolen by the Indians when a child, and kept by them fifteen years; then she was married to Captain Royall, and taught to read and write. She traveled much, and wrote several vituperatively amusing books. She settled down upon Washington society as editor of a newspaper called the "Washington Paul Pry" and of another, the "Huntress"; and she soon terrorized the place. No one in public office was spared, either in personal or printed abuse, if any offense or neglect was given to her. A persistent lobbyist, she was shunned like the plague by all congressmen. John Quincy Adams called her an itinerant virago. She was arraigned as a common scold before Judge William Cranch, and he sentenced her to be ducked in the Potomac River. She was, however,*

> *released with a fine, and appears to us to-day to have been*
> *insane—possibly through over-humored temper.*

Well: She might appear to be insane. Or she might appear to be, you know, a *journalist*. By all accounts, a good one: inquisitive, ruthless, unafraid to expose corruption and malfeasance in powerful institutions, and completely unwilling to bow to pressure, even when that pressure came from the highest offices in the nation.

The issue that nearly got Anne Royall dunked was separation of church and state, a favorite cause of hers. She'd exposed a plan by a prominent local minister to undermine it by pushing for the election of certain Christian candidates (a problem you might recall from, oh, *every* election you've ever voted in; it's why at least half of Congress spontaneously combusts when you mention Planned Parenthood) and protested the use of a firehouse—a federal building—to hold religious services. This sort of thing reduces Bill O'Reilly to blithering rage well into the twenty-first century. It was far less popular at the dawn of the nineteenth: People surrounded her house, taunted her, and threw pebbles at the windows until she stuck out her head and swore at them, hence the "scold" ruling. Strangely, this wasn't the worst thing that ever happened to Anne Royall at the hands of a disgruntled reader. One religious shopkeeper pushed her down a flight of stairs. Her opinions on religious zealotry were not significantly changed by the experience.

Which is to say: If John Quincy Adams was afraid of Anne Royall, he had good reason to be. The woman was a goddamn Terminator. She could not be scared, and she could not be stopped: Court rulings, public harassment, and attempts on her life notwithstanding, she kept publishing until her death at the age of eighty-five. She wasn't always right, or even admirable—she was on the wrong side of abolition, for one thing—but she was a historically formidable human being. And (Alice Morse Earle doesn't even mention this) she was quite probably the first female journalist in the United States.

And yet, for all that, she was remembered by successive generations as a crazy bitch who almost got thrown into a river. If it can happen to Anne Royall, who left a larger-than-average paper trail, one wonders how many other women's stories have been lost to us, through the strategic application of "insanity" diagnoses or public humiliation. How many firsts are still waiting for us, in those moldy, decaying old books, needing only a little careful dusting-off to come back to life?

"You say that this book is about trainwrecks," my friend Annette told me, when I'd been gushing a little too much about Mary Wollstonecraft again, "but these women don't seem wrecked. They seem *triumphant*."

It's true: Dig a little into even the most abject-seeming

wrecks and you usually find something to celebrate; some unique bit of ingenuity, or intelligence, hiding inside the official record of downfall and disgrace. Louise Augustine Gleizes, the much-photographed poster girl for hysteria, managed to escape La Salpêtrière in the middle of the night dressed as a boy and was never seen again; for all the time people spent staring at her face, nobody recognized it in a different context. Blanche Wittman's second act is even stranger: After Charcot died, and the staff of La Salpêtrière was regrettably forced to admit that she'd been sane all this time, she found work in their X-ray department. From there, she went on to befriend a woman by the name of Marie Curie, and became her lab assistant. The first Nobel Prize ever awarded to a woman would not have been possible without the work of someone whom art history has immortalized as a voluptuous, half-dressed lunatic.

But, more than that, writing about the trainwrecks of history gives the strange sensation of history itself becoming fluid. These women, almost to a one, seem as if they would fit into the twenty-first century more easily than their virtuous counterparts and critics; they seem like women dislocated in time.

Most obviously, Mary Wollstonecraft's scandalous sex life is now, by and large, the norm; not only are live-in relationships completely unremarkable, and late marriages ("late" here meaning "after age twenty-five") more common than ever, but the number of women who *never* marry has been rising steadily (8 percent in 1960 versus 17 percent in 2012), and single motherhood is increasingly something that women choose for themselves. The average mother today is older, more educated, and more single than she would have been even twenty years ago. In 2008, 41 percent of new mothers were unmarried (as compared to 28 percent in 1990) and, most significantly, this does not appear to be any kind of tragedy: 87 percent of all parents, single parents included, said that they chose to carry the pregnancy to term because of "the joy of having children." What made you a "prostitute" and a free-love radical in Wollstonecraft's time now just makes you a mom.

Likewise for Charlotte's forbidden crush, Plath's divorce, or even Valerie and Billie's fluid sexuality and relationships with women; all these things used to tar a woman as a deviant (and still might, in some evangelical churches) but increasingly, they're just part of life. Lindsay Lohan was scorned, laughed at, and subject to vile curiosity and speculation for dating Sam Ronson, but Miley Cyrus coming out of the closet might have been the one moment when the Internet *did* approve of her. Where *South Park* was able to release an episode like "Stupid Spoiled Whore Video Playset" in 2004 without fearing that America would rise up to defend Paris Hilton's virtue, its 2015 premiere, "Stunning and Brave," took as its premise the idea that people were *too eager* to say nice things about fellow reality-show diva Caitlyn Jenner. Yesterday's unforgivable transgressions are today's normal lives, and—unless we make our living out of saying hateful things about women, in which case, we might do some public complaining—we register them without a blink.

But the fact that sexual and political standards trend leftward over time is not news. In fact, some of the women who seemed boldest and most frightening in their time strike us as conservative now. When writing them up, I've tried to stress the ways they were ahead of the curve (it's hardly difficult to find negative coverage, after all) but it's easier for a modern reader to note that Wollstonecraft and Brontë failed to deal seriously with slavery, or to recoil from Solanas's crude, cruel caricatures of transgender women, than to see how strange they were in their historical moment. Time moves on, and the edges of gender theory now are miles away from anything that even our own consciousness-raising mothers and grandmothers imagined.

So it's particularly thrilling to bump into these women at the edges: to realize that some of them still have things to teach us today, might be right in ways we haven't even figured out yet.

In 2015, Mary Mitchell published an op-ed in the *Chicago Sun-Times*, arguing that prostitutes could not be raped: "When you agree to meet a strange man in a strange place for the purpose of having strange sex for money, you are putting yourself at risk for harm," she wrote. "It's tough to see this unidentified prostitute as a victim. And because this incident is being charged as a criminal sexual assault—when it's actually more like theft of services—it minimizes the act of rape."

I became aware of this article, not on its own merits, but because of the huge blowback surrounding it. One of the many nice things about feminism's evolution over the years is the fact that, by now, most forward-thinking people regard sex workers as human beings, and rape as a crime. *Salon*, *Jezebel*, *The Huffington Post*, and the other usual suspects all weighed in to disabuse Mitchell of her beliefs to the contrary.

"All survivors of rape—no matter who they are or what they do—deserve our support," wrote Anne Theriault at the *Daily Dot*, summing up the basic points of the response. "Rape is rape, whether or not you fit someone's profile of what a perfect victim looks like."

Strangely, this all came along just as I was reading up on Billie Holiday—who was, early in her life, a sex worker—and came upon this bit from *Lady Sings the Blues*:

"Even if you're a whore, you don't want to be raped," she had said. "A bitch can turn twenty-five hundred tricks a day, and she still don't want nobody to rape her."

It was the strangest thing. A couple of sentences, transcribed in 1956, had floated into my life, and they managed to sound exactly contemporary. Maybe, at the time, this had been part of the "harsh" language and "bitterness" that turned reviewers' stomachs, but every word of this (including, yes, Billie's casual use of "bitch" to mean "woman"—it was such a point of contention with her editors that she resorted to outright trolling them, writing "change 'bitch' to 'whore'" on one page of the manuscript) could show up on somebody's Twitter or Tumblr dashboard today.

If this keeps happening—if the disgraced women of history keep turning out to exist outside it, waiting for us on the road of progress decades or centuries ahead of where we expected them to stand—then one wonders what we'll discover about all the women we hate today: whether attracting scorn and disgrace is not a problem, but a distinction; whether every woman who viscerally upsets us is not in fact moving a bit faster than the rest of us, standing so far ahead we can't yet see her clearly, waiting for the world to catch up with what she knows.

•

Anatomy of a Trainwreck

THEROIGNE DE MERICOURT & MARIE ANTOINETTE

She was a singer. An entertainer. She was not wealthy growing up, but she had learned piano, and could sing very well, and could support herself on the stage. As all entertainers do, she found herself in the eyeline of several men, some powerful; one, an infantry officer, seduced her and vanished from her life. Their daughter died of smallpox. Another, an older man, a marquis, financed her lavishly on the condition that he kept complete control of her life. According to her, things were never physical. She fell in with other men, and the marquis became jealous, and she had to get rid of him.

All this came up as character evidence in her trial. Theroigne de Mericourt (a stage name; she was born Anne-Josephe Terwagne, in Marcourt) was being accused, among other things, of trying to overthrow the French government.

Nowadays, most of us think we know the French Revolution, if only on a rudimentary, seventh-grade-social-studies level. We know about the incompetent King Louis XIV; we know that the country was nearly bankrupt, and that the price of basic survival had gone up and up (bread, notoriously, was out of reach for most peasants); we know that, in the meantime, a group of idealistic young folks (journalists, law school students) had imbibed enough of the Enlightenment's ideals to foment a massive uprising, to tear down the walls of the Bastille and free the prisoners inside, to kill the king and queen, to overthrow aristocracy. And we also know that the plan to "overthrow the aristocracy" fell apart, almost at once, into a new and even more chaotic form of tyranny: there were street riots that became massacres, laws against "counter-revolutionary" sentiments and thought crimes, show trials and politically convenient executions (Camille Desmoulins, the young writer whose impassioned speech at a café launched the attack on the Bastille and therefore started the French Revolution proper, was executed early on for not being revolutionary enough), the infamous guillotine, and, ultimately, crazy old Robespierre, who not only tried to forge his own mandatory French religion, but also beheaded the very citizens he'd tried to free, sometimes just for saying things like "a fig for the Revolution!" (A charming expression from a more innocent time; today, we would say "I don't give a fuck.")

The French Revolution is either the Enlightenment's most glorious moment (to this day, left-wing magazines like *Jacobin* are named after Revolutionary factions; this is not unreasonable, given that the French Revolution invented the actual concept of "right" and "left" wings) or its most gruesome excess, depending on who you ask, and where they sit on the political spectrum. But one thing tends to remain the same, no matter who you're talking to: Everyone sees it as the work of radical men.

We tend to forget that, at the time, one of the more scandalous and frightening things about the Revolution was that women—assassin Charlotte Corday, writer Olympe de Gouges, or the everyday women who stormed Versailles and were often the most enthusiastic members of the audience at public executions—were taking an unprecedented role in public life. We tend to forget that, when it was actually happening, those who opposed the Revolution thought it made sense to blame Theroigne.

•   •   •

As an idealistic young woman living in Paris, she had hosted salons, where Revolutionary thinkers—Camille Desmoulins was a good friend—came to chat, and sometimes meet with publicists. The fact that Theroigne apparently slept with none of them raised a few eyebrows: "I have seen a number of wise men, who are widely respected, becoming amorously disposed towards this little person," wrote one newspaper, "although she rejected their advances with a Spartan pride, which they much laughed at subsequently, when they learned this exceedingly scrupulous beauty was simply a kept woman . . . The most innocent jests cause her to blush; the slightest provocation irritates her and yet she never spends her time in the company of anyone else but men."

If Theroigne was not looking to find a new man in these salons, what on Earth could she be doing? Well, among other things, she was attempting to plot a revolution that gave women a full and equal voice in the new France. It was an important cause for her, and one for which she would catch quite a lot of hell later in life. But her feminist politics escaped the attention of the press at the time, for the same reason that they escaped the attention of her fellow revolutionaries; nobody really cared about them. Feminism just wasn't on the agenda. It wasn't done.

What people cared about—cared about passionately, excessively, to a degree that confounded both logic and common sense—was what she *looked* like. Theroigne, the entertainer, had hit on the precise way to make her every statement both memorable and newsworthy: This strange, radical woman, people said, actually went around dressed as a *man.*

For her, it was a political statement: "I had always been extremely humiliated by the servitude and prejudices, under which the pride of men holds my oppressed sex." She dressed as a man to prove she was any man's equal. For the world at large, it was pure spectacle: Theroigne, a woman who consorted with men, spoke in public like men, tried to participate in government like a man, appeared before the world in a man's blood-red riding habit (though some reports said it was a black one, or maybe a white one— or was it purple, or green?) turning the accepted order of things upside-down with her image just as the Revolution was turning the world upside-down with its war on the divine right of kings.

She made such a perfect symbol, you could hardly blame people for seeing her everywhere. And they did: People claimed they saw Theroigne ride a cannon through the walls of the Bastille. (She wasn't even in Paris.) People claimed they saw Theroigne, at the head of a mob of women, storming Versailles. (She was sound asleep.) Her political enemies saw her as often as her supporters did, and often in a much uglier light: Plays were staged in which Theroigne fell madly in love with Deputy Populus (the name of an actual representative, but also meaning "The Populace"—Theroigne, whose refusal to sleep with her male colleagues had once been newsworthy, was now said to be sleeping with literally every man in France). One report saw a heavily pregnant Theroigne give birth on the floor of the National Assembly: "This nymph is a trollop, and obsessed by men; indeed, every representative may fairly claim to be the father of her child." Like Wollstonecraft, mere prose was not enough to express the extent of people's dislike for her. There were also, God help us, the poems:

> *Theroigne in the district, as well as in the brothel*
> *has used her various talents to experiment*
> *with her tongue and arse, which are so precious to France*
> *her name will live forever.*

Presumably it rhymes in French.

People liked seeing Theroigne. They just didn't like hearing her. While all these articles were being written, Theroigne's *actual* attendance at the National Assembly was spent getting into increasingly futile debates over assertions such as "the rights of a man over his wife and, likewise, the rights of a father over his children are those of a protector over his protégés," a very left-wing Revolutionary statement which Theroigne was the sole attendee to protest. By the time she was picked up and interrogated by the Austrian government (a process that involved an attempted rape), not only was she *not* a major part of the Revolutionaries' plans—"I cannot bring myself to admit that she could have played as important a role in the events in Paris as has been attributed to her," was the official finding—she had more or less dropped out:

"I left the French Revolution without too much regret," she said, "for every day I had suffered some degree of harassment in the public galleries of the National Assembly; there were invariably some aristocrats who, being offended by my zeal and my frankness, would heap sarcasms on me . . . while the patriots, instead of encouraging me and treating me justly, ridiculed me. This is the plain and simple truth. I was therefore, so to speak, disgusted."

Strangely—yet, somehow, inevitably—the one woman in France with whom Theroigne had the most in common was also the one woman she most relentlessly opposed: Marie Antoinette, the Austrian queen, the face of the decadent aristocracy at its worst. "L'Autrichienne," as the Revolutionary press called her. It was a clever little play on words from Theroigne's progressive brotherhood, *chien* meaning *dog*: Marie Antoinette, the Austrian Bitch.

"Let them eat cake?" She never said it. That necklace she supposedly stole? She was framed. Her husband was most likely asexual—Louis refused to sleep with Marie for the first seven years of their marriage, and there are no reports of his ever having a mistress or male partner; this, despite the fact that the French court was so sexually tolerant that "Official Mistress" was an actual job title—and she did eventually take one lover, the Swedish Count Abel von Fersen, though some will say there's no firm proof she ever had sex with him, either. But this was hardly enough for the people, or for their preferred media, which constructed entire *Game of Thrones*–level plotlines for Marie Antoinette daily: She was a lesbian, she slept with every lady in the court, she was sexually insatiable, she slept with every *man* in the court, she *particularly* slept with her brother-in-law, all the royal heirs were bastards.

Not only were Theroigne and Marie said to have equally Brobdingnagian sex lives—one pamphlet, which claimed to be the "confessions" of Marie Antoinette herself, has her describe herself as "barbaric queen, adulterous wife, woman without morals, soiled by crime and debauchery," and goes on to cheerfully note that she is "a despicable prostitute"; still another claimed that, among the supporters of monarchy, "all its members have drawn from the vagina of the Austrian Woman . . . [that] infectious cavern is the receptacle of all vices, where each comes and takes his required dose"—Marie was lucky enough to have pornography produced in her name, for people who needed an aid to the imagination. One portrait, entitled "The Royal Dildo," shows the Queen happily greeting General Lafayette as he rides toward her on a disembodied dick the size of a pony.

With leftists like these, it was no wonder that Theroigne had trouble getting a hearing. But sex wasn't all of it. Sex was most of it, but not all. The Austrian Bitch was also *Madame Deficit*, the greedy, decadent drain on an entire country's wealth; if the French government was broke, it was because Marie Antoinette broke it by doing too much shopping. Granted, Marie was hardly the heroic type. She had only two jobs: First, to secure an alliance between the French and the Austrians by getting married, and second, to secure the continuity of the French monarchy by having children. She did both dutifully, if not always well. And unlike Theroigne, her outfits were not chosen as political protests. But they sure did enrage people: While the French people were starving, Marie Antoinette constructed an entire fake farm and posed for portraits dressed as a milkmaid.

Theroigne slept with everybody. Marie slept with everybody. Theroigne was the living symbol of a political party's outrageousness. Marie was the living symbol of a political party's decadence. If you were on Theroigne's side, she was a shining light, an "Amazon of Liberty," a heroine. If you were on Marie's side, she was a beautiful princess, a persecuted mother, our rightful queen. No matter which side you chose, the other was a disgraceful whore and a symbol of everything wrong with the world. For Theroigne and for Marie, the same stereotypes always came up, and for Theroigne and for Marie, the press held to one simple rule: The facts never mattered. What mattered was the story.

Somehow, in the midst of the French Revolution, we, as humans, managed to stumble onto one more crucial insight. The media could advance any political agenda it wanted, and whip up people's emotions in any direction they felt necessary, and they didn't even have to tell the truth to do it, *as long as the other side was projected onto the body of an unlikable woman.* There and then, in Theroigne and Marie, in war and blood and turmoil, the contemporary trainwreck was forged.

May God have mercy on their souls.

Trainwrecks end in blood or obscurity, and Theroigne and Marie are no exception. Marie's end is more famous: Imprisoned, sick, bereaved, given a show trial in which, in one last sickening twist, the legend of her promiscuity broadened to include accusations that she was molesting her infant son. She was beheaded, her famous last words—"Pardon me, sir, I did not mean to do it"; she had stepped on the executioner's foot—seemingly standing in for any number of real or imagined sins. The next day, the Revolutionary newspaper *Pere Duchesne* reported "the greatest of all the joys of the Pere Duchesne, having with his own eyes seen the head of the [Queen] separated from her fucking tart's neck."

Theroigne has no last words. Or she has thousands, which were never recorded. Theroigne was greeted as a hero, when the Austrians let her go, and became a more potent symbol than ever. She immediately squandered it, as she always did, on her ridiculous "rights for women" thing. At one point, a man in the Assembly mentioned enjoying the chance to hear her speak at a café, upon which his male colleagues started laughing at him. Theroigne, unfortunately, was in the audience, and caused a minor scandal by climbing out of the women's section and physically throwing herself at the bench. And, at a moment when the party was purifying itself (which meant, naturally, killing moderates to preserve true leftism) Theroigne issued a pamphlet warning against Revolutionary infighting: "I propose that each section appoint six women citizens, the most virtuous and the most serious for their age, who would have the task of reconciling and uniting the men citizens," she wrote.

This particular choice—moderatism! Centrism! Opposing the true brotherhood of the Left!—was the one that could not be forgiven. Theroigne was taken aside and physically whipped. Her clothes were half torn off. It is probable that they meant to kill her. Marat, then a hero to this contingent, pulled her out of the center of the dogpile, and it was believed that he saved her life.

The people who whipped Theroigne were women. Every report that we have about Theroigne de Mericourt going mad agrees that it started here: After she'd done so much, risked so much, been imprisoned, been mocked, been sexually assaulted, all for a female Revolution, the people who finally, fully kicked Theroigne out of the Revolution, the people who actually made an attempt on her life, were *other women*. She simply never got over it.

She retired, for good this time. She started writing her memoirs. The next time anyone heard about her, she had been locked in a mental institution by her brother. She was writing pleading letters to the Revolution's leaders, asking to be released—"I have neither paper nor light, in fact I have nothing; even so, I must be free in order to write; it is impossible for me to do anything here," she wrote to St. Just—but they were not answered.

The Revolution was falling apart. The Revolutionaries had killed the monarchs, and then the leftist Revolutionaries had killed the moderate ones, and then the remaining leftists had killed the slightly more moderate leftists, and, sure enough, it had gotten to the point at which Robespierre had just started killing people for cursing, and so they had to kill Robespierre, and they also had to kill St. Just for supporting Robespierre, and by the time Theroigne was begging the Revolution to come and save her, nothing really held it all together any more. Everyone, it turned out, had someone else that they felt like killing. So Theroigne had actually been right, that you could overdo it with the infighting—this was *twice* now, when you counted her women's-rights obsession; chalk up another big mark in the Wins column for Theroigne—but once again, it did her no good. There was no one left who could save her.

The next time Theroigne de Mericourt was presented with paper and pen, by her doctor, she scarcely recognized them: "She outlined a few words, but she never managed to form a whole sentence. She never gave any sign of hysteria," he wrote.

By then, years later, she was where women like her always wound up: Theroigne was in La Salpêtrière. She was a remarkable case, this woman, a striking example of the madness that had led people to believe there could be a Revolution. Theroigne did not know what year it was; she asked for people (Robespierre, St. Just) who were long since dead. She appeared to give speeches to no one, using words no one used any more: "She acted as if she were involved in very important matters; she smiled at the people around her . . . [she] spoke to herself in a low voice, using disjointed sentences composed of words such as 'fortune,' 'liberty,' 'committee,' 'revolution,' 'wretches,' 'decree,' 'ruling,' etc. She had a real grievance against the moderates," her doctor wrote.

But this was, more or less, her obituary. And it was one last inaccurate thing written about Theroigne: Esquirol, the head of Salpêtrière, recorded for posterity that she "gave herself to various leaders of the party," was instrumental in most of the Revolution's key events, and that "she was to be seen with a red cap on her head, a sabre at her side, a pike in her hand, commanding an army of women." Then he recorded the results of her autopsy: Pneumonia. He cut her skull open to check for malformations of the brain (you had to do the research, it might help eventually). And then Theroigne was done. The woman no one wanted to listen to, finally finished giving one long speech that no one wanted to hear.

●

Sexual overabundance, emotional overabundance, all the too-muchness and too-bigness that comes with being a flaming wreck of a woman: Is there anything, really, wrong with it?

I'm not talking about being *hurt*, here; I'm not talking about the damage to body and mind we associate with addiction or mental illness. I'm talking about *moral* wrong, evil, the choice to make the world worse for the people in it. Getting addicted is the result of a bad decision, in many cases, but bad decisions aren't evil; we all make them, every day. And you can get sick, get injured, you can even die, without that being inherently immoral: Hurting yourself, or more accurately, having a disease that hurts you, is painful for you and for your loved ones, but it is not the same as intentionally victimizing another person or a group of people. We don't picket people with diabetes. We don't tell cancer patients that it makes us sick to look at them. And hating illnesses doesn't cure them. If you want people to stop being heartbroken about mentally ill and addicted loved ones, or if you want people to stop being mentally ill and addicted, decriminalizing drug use and getting everyone to a nice, free, socialized-medicine-provided doctor is probably your best bet.

So, I ask again, what is *wrong* with being too much? With being too big? With being openly sexual, openly emotional—with having "no calmness or content except when the needs of [your] individual nature were satisfied," as Martineau wrote of Wollstonecraft—or even with being openly unhappy?

Only this: Insisting on the needs of your individual nature, being unquiet and unhappy when those needs are not satisfied, requires that you have an individual nature to begin with. And it requires that you not be ashamed of it.

The trainwreck's "good" sister, the feminine ideal floating just under the surface of our derision, gets more disquieting the more you look at her. She is a hollow doll, all reaction and no action: Completely asexual unless it is necessary for her to want sex, unable to love without being loved in return, unable to raise her voice or cry or suffer, for fear that the noise might bother somebody. Unable, it seems, to feel much at all, except concern for how others *want* her to feel, and eagerness to fulfill their expectations.

Consider the qualities that made Britney, that most impossibly Good of all Good Girls, so appealing to the music industry: "In all that she did, Britney gave the distinct impression that if an adult says do something, you do it," said Chuck Yerger, principal of the Mickey Mouse School where Britney was educated. "She truly felt that all adults and people in authority were good people, who had her best interests at heart." Max Martin, who co-wrote her career-making hit ". . . Baby One More Time," was drawn to her because of his recent experiences with more self-motivated pop stars: "Max said, 'She's fifteen years old; I can make the record I want to make, and use her qualities appropriately, without her telling me what to do.' Which is kind of what happened."

Consider this, and then consider the ever-obvious fact that even Britney couldn't give enough; all the trust and obedience in the world couldn't make her totally absent from her own life, or take her inner conflicts away.

The good girl, the un-trainwreck, is feminine selflessness, taken to its most literal extreme; there is no self, no *there*, except as a reflection of someone else's wishes. She never makes mistakes, and she never has regrets, because she never does anything unless she is asked to do it. She is so entirely cleansed of neediness, irrationality, and inner conflict that the average woman cannot imitate her even in silence: Women who go silent about their needs, it turns out, still have needs. They're silent because they're repressing what they have to say. The ideal woman has a silence that arises from never wanting to speak about anything at all. And what living thing could be *that* passive, *that* quiet? Why *is* it, really, that we fixate on all of those Dead Blondes and Tragic Princesses? After looking at her long enough—the good woman, the ideal woman, the woman the trainwreck isn't—you get the disturbing impression that she's not a woman at all. She is a woman's corpse.

And the trainwreck is crazy because we're *all* crazy— because, in a sexist culture, being female is an illness for which there is no cure. We are all too sexual, or sexual in the wrong ways. We are all too emotional, or emotional about the wrong things. We are all prone to think and feel and want things that other people don't like or can't tolerate or don't want to give us, at least sometimes, because we are *ourselves*, and therefore *not those people*—because there's a *there*, an "I," a self that is not and cannot be determined by what the world wants or needs at any given time. Everyone faces that problem, at some point. But women, as a group, are far more likely to feel that having their own minds, rather than the mind of the person they're talking to, is a sign that something is wrong.

What the trainwreck does, why she so frequently turns up ahead of us, is to act as if nothing is wrong. Loudly. Whether through conscious political engagement or sheer force of personality, she presents the world with a big, loud, unavoidable abundance of Self. Her body wants what it wants (food, alcohol, drugs, sex) and we all know it. Her heart feels what it feels (love, grief, rage, joyful abandon) and we all hear about it. Her opinions are so pronounced, and so gleefully indifferent to disagreement, that you can knock her down a staircase, lock her up, or throw her in the river without changing them. She makes mistakes, and she makes enemies, but no matter how many of them pile up in her wake, the trainwreck *is*. And not all the social conventions, laws, cruel jokes, or disapproving glances in the world can make her other than what she is. She winds up being right because, simply by virtue of overflowing all boundaries, she flows over those barriers to freedom that history and justice will naturally erode in time.

The trainwreck is alive. And for a woman to be fully
alive is revolutionary.

This has been a book of female confessions: Humiliating, private things that women either brought themselves
to publish or had published for them, or that were wrung
out of them under duress. So here, as a form of penance
for repeating all that dirt, is my own confession. I spend
pretty much every day of my life talking about and advocat-
ing feminism. And yet I have, throughout my life, felt very
wretched, for a very large portion of my day, because I could
not be a "strong feminist woman."

Strong feminist women, for example, don't cry hysteri-
cally over breakups. Strong feminist women don't even have
breakups, as far as I can tell; they have functional egalitarian
partnerships of their choosing (if their sexual and emotional
fulfillment is best served by monogamy), and when it's
time for things to end, they settle things with a firm hand-
shake and an all-around congratulations to both partners
on an A-OK job. Strong feminist women also have great,
healthy body images; they do not, as I do, recoil from every
known photo of themselves. Strong feminist women don't
have trouble paying the rent, probably because they're so
busy breaking the glass ceiling at their various workplaces;
strong feminist women don't publish their opinions, then
feel guilty and horrible about themselves because someone

disagrees with those opinions. Strong feminist women have probably never deleted twenty Tweets about Taylor Swift in a row. I have. I do. I am not a strong feminist woman, as it turns out; I'm a person, and sometimes I do good stuff, and sometimes I don't. It's as easy as that, or it should be, if I didn't spend so much time feeling horrible about it all.

I am not a special case, I don't think. Every day brings me new evidence that women, by and large, do not like themselves very much: their ambition gaps, their orgasm gaps, their impostor syndromes, their poor body images, their endless variety of real or perceived failures, including their failures to feel good about who and what they are. Their trainwrecks, and their need for trainwrecks; the enduring, self-loathing need to find someone about whom they can say *well, at least I'm not that girl.*

But, in the context of trainwreck media, a female self-confidence gap is not only predictable, it's practically unavoidable. We can't spend twelve hours a day mainlining ideas of sexual or emotional or aging or ill women as monsters, messes, and freaks, then expect to wake up feeling beautiful and confident in the morning. Every "ugly" photo of Amy Winehouse, every nasty word typed about Azealia Banks in a comment section, is going to come back the next time we're vulnerable, and take yet another chunk out of our ability to believe that we can screw up and still be basically worthwhile.

So here's the moral of all these tales, the monster at the

end of the book: I may not be a strong feminist woman. And, if you are a woman, and reading this book, it's entirely possible that *you* aren't a strong feminist woman, either. Because the fact is, I've spent a while looking at the lives of the strongest, most feminist women in history. The icons; the immortal geniuses; the women to whom we are all meant to aspire. And the thing is? There's not a strong feminist woman among them.

Charlotte Brontë was a genius, whose work has resonated for centuries as an example of female intellect and expressive power. Her letters to Constantin Heger are some of the stupidest things I've ever read, a masterful, two-year-long demonstration of one woman's inability to absorb the fact that the guy she liked *did not like her.* Mary Wollstonecraft was over a century ahead of her time on women's education, and twice as far ahead on women's sexual freedom. She *still* thought she'd rather drown than not have a boyfriend. Harriet Jacobs was possibly one of the bravest women who ever lived. She survived unspeakable atrocity, thanks only to her own daring, ingenuity, and resilience, and published one of the most important political documents of her age. And she was afraid that "educated people" would make fun of her grammar.

She was scared, but she did it. That's all being strong is, apparently: being scared, or flawed, or weak, or capable (under the right circumstances) of astonishing acts of stupidity. And then going out and doing it all anyway. Trying, every morning, to be the woman you want to be, regardless of how often you manage to fall short of your own high expectations.

Feminine ideals are a strange business. They seem to have been constructed, for most of history, to rule out pretty much every living woman. And "strong feminist woman," though it's managed to kick the can a few yards down the road—now you don't just have to be literally perfect at all of your relationships; you also get a job, and it turns out you need to be perfect at that, *too*—can, all too easily, turn into yet another trap. Applied the right way, it can allow us to applaud each other for what we do manage to get right. Applied in the age of trainwrecks, it can become yet another mile-high yardstick, against which women measure themselves and each other, and invariably come up short.

We have been punishing women for doing public life "the wrong way" for as long as women have had public lives. And, as women have pushed ever more inexorably into the public sphere—as the movements of Theroigne and Mary and Harriet and Billie and Valerie gained momentum, and pushed more women, of more sexualities and races and class backgrounds, ever further into the public eye and into positions of power—we have developed ever more technologies and means by which to insult them. This may make entering the public sphere dangerous, and painful. But it is, perhaps, less painful to be punished for what you do than to punish yourself by never doing anything at all.

"It is perfectly simple," Theroigne once said, "and you should even be forewarned against it, that they will marshal the carpers and the hired hacks in an attempt to keep us back, using the weapons of ridicule and calumny, and all the ignoble means that base men employ . . . I would urge you yet again: let us raise ourselves to the height of our destinies; let us break our chains; at last the time is ripe for Women to emerge from their shameful nullity, where the ignorance, pride and injustice of men had kept them enslaved for so long a time[.]"

Theroigne was right. If you are a woman, and you make yourself visible in the world, they will always marshal the carpers, and (if you're lucky) some hired hacks, to insult you back into silence. But she was also correct that these are ignoble means, and base men employ them; base men have, in fact, been employing those tools for centuries, apparently without ever getting even a little bit more imaginative as to their uses. And they are easy tools to break.

Because the only big secret that all that ridicule can reveal—the only big weapon anyone has against you—is that you're human. Fucked-up, a bit. Imperfect, yes. In this, you are like every great human who has ever lived, male and female alike. If you're slutty, well, Mary Wollstonecraft was pretty slutty. If you're needy, my God, Charlotte Brontë's needs could devour a person alive. If you're mean, or self-destructive, or crazy, I assure you, Billie Holiday managed to record "Strange Fruit" while being spectacularly self-destructive, and Sylvia Plath wrote *Ariel* while being both crazy and very, very mean. The world is still better with those works in it. Humanity is still lucky that those particular women existed, and that, despite their deep flaws and abundance of raw humanity, they stood up and said what they had to say.

But maybe we should give Theroigne the last word here. God knows, she's had to wait for it.

"If we wish to preserve our liberty," Theroigne said, "we must be prepared to do the most sublime things."

The first item on that list, and the greatest liberty you can claim, lies in deciding that you—human, fuck-up, mess, trainwreck that you are—may well be capable of the sublime.

Conclusion

THE VIEW FROM
THE TRACKS

A fourteen-year-old girl in Florida wakes up to find "SLUT" painted on her driveway. Her MySpace page has been drawing the wrong kind of attention. It's not the word that's the problem: It's the fact that they know where she lives.

A woman gives birth to octuplets in California. It's discovered that she's on public assistance, and that she has six other children. "Octomom" is the joke of the year. Her sanity and resemblance to Angelina Jolie become matters of public speculation. She's offered a chance to make ends meet by starring in porn.

A woman Tweets a picture of herself dressed as a Boston Marathon bombing victim for Halloween. The name and address of her employer are uncovered in the comment section of a sports blog. She is fired almost immediately. She receives rape threats and threats to bomb the houses of her friends and family. Someone found them, too.

A PR worker tweets a racist joke before boarding an airplane. She becomes a trending topic globally. When the plane lands, someone from the hashtag is there to greet her. They knew where she was. Everyone knew where she was. Anyone could have been waiting for her, there on the other side.

A teenage girl is raped by boys who post a videotape of it on social media in Ohio.

A teenage girl is raped by boys who post a videotape of it on social media in New York.

A teenage girl is raped by boys who post a videotape of it on social media, again.

And again.

And again.

A teenage girl posts a video about her rape and subsequent suicide attempt on social media. By the time we see it, she's gone.

There is a final step to this process—beyond celebrity blogs, beyond twenty-four-hour news coverage, beyond celebrities at all. You could say that we've started to go easier on famous people, in the last few years. (Ariana Grande, who landed on a most-hated-celebrities list for licking a doughnut, might disagree.) But the fact is, if we've backed off on famous women at all, it's because we don't really need them any more. Why would we? We have each other.

The boom in surveillance and communications technologies that turned famous people from distant, nearly mythical objects of adoration into professionals who stay in contact with their fan bases twenty-four hours a day—thus allowing us to see them, un-Photoshopped warts and all—had another, even more radical effect. We are now able to see our fellow citizens, just as clearly as we ever saw the stars. Friends, family, Katy Perry, or some woman with too many babies or a bad outfit or an annoying Twitter feed in Detroit: It's all the same, all perfectly visible, on the twenty-four-hour feed of human flaws and failures to which many of us now stay plugged in for most of the day.

Celebrities, even in the late-2000s heyday of Britney and Amy and Whitney—the age when it seemed that privacy was definitively over, and the distance separating us from them was hair-thin at best—always had certain disadvantages, as targets. For one thing, it was a big investment: To knock a famous woman down, you had to spend years building her up and getting to know her, and by that point she was bound to have more than a few die-hard fans. For another thing, celebrities were professionals, even when they didn't act like it: It was their *job* to be public, and to sell themselves to the public. So they always had teams, managers, fellow professionals who could coach them through their mistakes and at least attempt to turn around the narrative. Celebrities, even when the verdict against them was seemingly unanimous, had power. Their annihilation could never be total.

Except, of course, that for Whitney and Amy, it was. And, of course, after we'd had fun with them all throughout the Perez Hilton Administration, they wound up dying within seven months of each other, and just as the '10s started. Guilt no doubt played a role here.

But if you couldn't go after celebrities and feel good about yourself—or if you couldn't go after celebrities and *win*, which for some people may be the same thing—you could always go after the "LEAVE BRITNEY ALONE" guy. And people did. Lots of them. Face it: When I typed those words, you knew exactly who I meant. And you probably remember finding it funny.

But lots of people found it funny simply because he was a relatively feminine-seeming person, who wore makeup and was heavily invested in a woman's feelings, and was in obvious pain. And those people tend to find it equally funny to go after women.

Civilian women make better, bigger, messier trainwrecks. They just do. There's no track record, no prior investment. When they fuck up, their fuck-ups can become the whole story: You *knew* the Boston Marathon Costume Girl, or Octomom, or Tiger Mom, or Crying YouTube Kid With Weird Dad (who transitioned a few years later, but who was likely treated so viciously because people saw him as a little girl—there was only one thing folks had in mind when they called him "slut" and went to look for "nudes"), but you didn't know anything about them before their moments of infamy. Their worst moments were all they'd ever been.

Also, normal people don't have "teams"; they don't have defense strategies prepared. When they fumble and fluster and break down and dig themselves in deeper—which they almost invariably do—they're doing it for *real*, because they're not famous, and they don't know how to be, and "stage a comeback when the world hates you" is quite possibly the single hardest task with which to start learning fame. The effective comeback from ignominy is something you learn when you're at grad school levels of Famous: Robert-Downey-Junior-in-*Iron-Man*, Britney-Does-Vegas levels of Good at Being Famous. These people? Some of them are literally children. Not only can't they rebound from global infamy, they couldn't open a mall.

You can do the trainwreck quick, clean, easy, if you pick them off social media. You can get in and out, in a week tops, with a definitive casualty and (usually) no visible blood on anyone's hands. It performs the same function that trainwrecks always have: It keeps women convinced that there's something wrong with them, and afraid to step out of line. More afraid than ever before, in fact. All those years, you thought you were just standing around, waiting to see the trains collide with something. Now you look down and find out that you're standing on the tracks.

"The Internet is mean" is a pretty well-rehearsed truism, and frankly, a bad one. Dig into "the Internet is mean," and usually you find some variety of "people are too sensitive these days," which itself is usually hiding "Why can't women take a compliment?" or "I should be able to say the n-word," and ultimately, the inescapable conclusion is that people often claim that the *Internet* is mean because *they* would like to be much, much meaner, preferably toward their least-favorite oppressed groups.

The Internet, in and of itself, is not mean. "The Internet" is millions of people, and we don't all check in with each other to set the day's agenda when we log on. But when "the Internet" has an established pattern of fixating on and demonizing specifically female people, we can identify a real problem. It's an old, unsexy, thoroughly established problem that we persist in finding strange and inexplicable every time a new communication technology is invented to perpetuate it.

Twitter is not mean; Tumblr is not mean; Facebook is not mean; blogs, cable news channels, magazines, and newspapers are not mean. *Misogyny is mean.* Misogyny is the art and craft of being particularly mean to women, and treating them worse than you treat men, because you think they are not as good as male people. The Internet did not start this fight; it only enables us to have it on a new scale. GamerGate started the first time a man ever put a gag on a woman and paraded her through town for criticizing him too harshly. Making fun of crying, feminine people in YouTube videos started when we invented the concept of hysteria. "Revenge porn" began at the moment that men decided that women's sexuality was disgusting, and that women should be humiliated for it, which (if you go by the Bible, anyway) happened more or less immediately after God created Heaven and Earth. Page 1, God creates Eve. Page 2, we all have to wear clothes now because Eve is awful. I doubt it's a strictly factual account, but these attitudes are deeply embedded.

Which means that our only hope of changing them, of ending the wrecks, lies not in stopping or even changing the Internet—even with the best blocking functions, report-abuse functions, real-name transparency protocols, and twenty-four-hour moderation in the world, hate (to quote *Jurassic Park*) finds a way—but in changing ourselves, and our definitions of womanhood. We have to stop believing that when a woman does something we don't like, we are qualified and entitled to punish her, violate her, or ruin her life. We have to change our ideas of what a "good" woman, or a "likable" woman, or simply a "woman who can leave her house without fearing for her life because she is a woman," can be.

And we do have to do it. All of us. Each of us for our

own sake. Maybe you're not worried, right now; maybe you're doing all of the right things, and none of the wrong ones. Maybe you think you could spot the danger coming, stop yourself before you made your big mistake. Maybe, right now, you feel perfectly safe. For you, there is no train coming. No sign that you might get hit.

But we had train tracks in my town, when I was growing up. There's something they taught us in school about them. There must have been accidents, because they repeated this very often: Trains move much faster than you think they do. Trains are also surprisingly quiet, for objects of their size. You can *never* stand on the train tracks. Not ever. Not if you want to live. By the time you hear the train coming, you are always hearing it too late.

There is the potential for redemption in all this. The same tools that we use to observe and police and judge each other have also given us the ability to resist that judgment, and potentially to expose it for the fallacy that it is.

I run into quite a lot of women online. I am given access to an endless stream of inner monologues, all female, all different. It's why I go there in the first place—an endless world of women, almost none of whom I would otherwise know, all giving me the world as it is from inside their skin. Checking Twitter, at 6:49 a.m. on a Tuesday, I see, at random: A Scottish PhD in Digital Sociology, a cul-

ture editor for *Buzzfeed UK*, a world-renowned Indian envi-
ronmentalist and anti-globalization activist, a novelist and
Springsteen fan from Brooklyn, and an independent theatre
director in Washington, D.C. This is an incomplete list. The
women I can see are (again, at random, in one moment of
time) discussing a potential biopic of Pakistan's first woman
firefighter, showing off Twitter bots they created, sharing
pictures of their hair back-combed into beehives, saying
they've really grown to like Lianne La Havas's second album, and admitting that they use cartoon-character glasses
to serve wine. And this list, too, is incomplete. These are
the wee hours of the morning, and my Twitter feed is not
yet crowded.

Granted, the #1 trending topic is still a debate about
whether Rihanna is a Bad Role Model for Women—those
debates seem to arise every two weeks, and the verdict for
Rihanna is never favorable—but you begin to see my point.
There are literally millions of women, speaking in public, at
this moment in time. Each woman gets to tell me exactly
what she wants me to know, in her own words, at any hour
of the day or night. I have personally come to know hundreds, maybe thousands of women in this fashion. I like
some, dislike others, and am entirely neutral much of the
time. But these women I hear about? The Good Women?
The Ideal Women? Or the truly, unilaterally, unfixably *horrible* women? The Trainwrecks?

The thing is, I've never seen one. Not in real life. Not

in the wild. As far as I can tell—and I have more evidence, and more access to it, than I would have had at any other point in history—they don't exist. Even the women who seem Good or Bad at first glance tend to fragment into something more complicated and ambiguous if you look at them long enough. Women are not symbols of superhuman virtue. Women are not symbols of all that is disgusting and corrupt. Women, it turns out, are not symbols of anything, other than themselves.

And if I can see this, given only the ability to read and an Internet connection, then women throughout the world can see it as well. It's as simple as opening a window. All the standards we've been trying to chase, all the Goodness we shame ourselves for not having, all the Badness we impute to each other in anger or in fear . . . it just isn't real. None of it was ever real. It was something we believed in, like the flat earth, or curing diseases by balancing humours, before we had the tools to see how things really worked. All the women we were supposed to be, all the women we feared being: They never existed. The only thing that exists is *us*, in a world where there are no normal girls.

There's a dream I had, writing this book. I'm alone in a room, a high school locker room. People come in—every person I know will eventually come into this room—and I hand them a black marker.

This is my punishment, for everything I've done wrong in life. Each person is allowed to write one new word on my body—the worst thing they've ever thought about me, or wanted for me, summed up. "Die," "slut," "cunt." These are popular choices. An ex-boyfriend writes some crack about my body. He takes care to write it on my back, so I can't see it—he knows I'll be more bothered that way. Parents write "disappointment." Strangely, none of these hurts as much as the people who refuse to write anything. They just stare at me and walk away. They don't hate me. They just don't care.

It has to go on this way, until there's no more room to write. Until I'm completely covered in other people's assessments of me. Then, they take me to the water and hold me under. Like the "common scolds" were held under the water, to cure them of running off at the mouth. Like Whitney, falling into her bathtub, all alone.

I'm not scared of this, strangely enough. It could be bad, but I still don't know why they're doing it. They either intend to drown me, or to save me. Either I'll die of being hated, or all the words, all the harsh judgments and insults I've accumulated throughout my lifetime, will just wash away.

With all that we can do to each other, these days, it still seems like this is the choice at hand. We can drown in it, the judgment and hatred we have for each other. We can tank women's lives, hold them under until they shut up or stop breathing. Or we can let it wash away.

I don't know how you feel. I don't know what you're writing onto the women in your life. I don't know what's been written on you. But this is what I hope for you: that when they take you to the water, you come out clean again. That nothing they write on you can define you. I hope we all wind up back on dry land, clean and new as morning.

Acknowledgments

Do not skip these acknowledgments.

I always used to skip the acknowledgements! I thought they were self-indulgent. The author says some nice things about their parents, tells you which famous people they know, I flip the page because of how bored I am, and it's over. Now, I know they're more like the credits of a movie: Without them, you think George Clooney just came up with witty things to say while robbing a casino, and cameras happened to be there at the time.

George Clooney is talented, but he can't do everything. A lot of people go into making George Clooney look good. These are the people who made me look good.

This book would not exist without Miranda Popkey, who told me to write one, and worked with me on several early chapters. It also would not exist without Taylor Sperry, my editor, who took it on, and edited out the terrible parts. There were some very terrible parts. Thank you, Taylor. Melissa Flashman, my agent, brokered the deal, and is similarly wonderful. Stuart Calderwood fixed my grammar. Melville House, generally, took a risk on me. Their generosity has been astonishing.

Emily Gould, Clay Shirky, Kate Harding, Andi Zeisler, Irin Carmon, and Lindy West took time out of their day to say nice things about me without being paid for it, so that I could put it on the book and sucker you into buying a copy. Please do not blame them if you did not like this book. I asked them to do it.

All of the women in the "Anatomy of a Trainwreck" sections, with the exception of Marie Antoinette, have published books or essays themselves. I'm deeply indebted to them, and to all the biographers who made it possible for me to study their lives. If you liked any of those sections, please, please seek out and read the work of those women: For all that has been said about them, and for all that I've said about them, they still need and deserve to be heard in their own words.

I used to have a Wordpress blog. The only reason I'm not "some person with a Wordpress blog" is that people read it, and linked to it. If you did that: I thank you. If you regret doing that: I understand.

My husband, Brian, took care of the apartment while I stared at my computer being upset about Theroigne de Mericourt. He is an extremely patient man.

My stepfather and my brother have put up with me being

in their family with only minor amounts of complaining. They, too, are very patient men.

My mother stole one of my complimentary book galleys, but gave me twenty-five dollars for it. We then spent it on champagne. Her only request was that I not include anything embarrassing about her in the book. Sorry, Mom!

My mom also took me to a drugstore, when I was six, to buy me a notebook, because I said I wanted to write a book. Her belief that I would actually write one has never wavered since that day.

Hey, Mom: Here it is.

Notes

CHAPTER 1: SEX

4   **"Can we *please* have one fucking day away":** "Britney and Kevin: Going Down Above Street Level," *Gawker*, July 24, 2004.

5   **In 2004, Britney Spears:** "Britney Spears, Paris Hilton Most Googled," Ed Oswald, *BetaNews*, December 23, 2004.

5   **Salomon sued her for defamation:** "Next Legal Tango in Paris Tape Case," *New York Daily News*, November 9, 2003.

6   **"continuously cough[ing] up semen":** "Stupid Spoiled Whore Video Playset," Wikipedia.

6   **"It annoys me that so many people assume something":** "When Piers Met Paris," *GQ*, July 23, 2010.

6   **"What is with these twenty-something girls":** "Britney Spears Upskirt, Take Two: Now with Virtually Nothing Left to the Imagination," *Gawker*, November 28, 2006.

7   **In addition to the 2012 "upskirt," in 2008, hacker Josh Holly:** "Miley Cyrus hacker faces 13 years in jail after pleading guilty to fraud and hacking charges," *The Daily Mail*, August 2, 2011.

8   **"For Miley Cyrus to be a 'good girl' is now a business decision":** "Topless Photo Creates Concern over Disney Franchise," *New York Times*, April 28, 2015.

8   **"It's wrong for Miley to have agreed to play the child":** "Miley Cyrus Is an Oversexed Trainwreck Waiting to Happen!," *Hollywood Life*.

9   SPLIT TRIGGERED BY ANTICS WITH MILEY: "Robin/Paula Split Triggered by Antics with Miley," *TMZ*, February 27, 2014.

9   **"molesting of Robin Thicke":** "Stubborn Persistence of Pop," *New York Times*, August 26, 2013.

9   **"Miley Cyrus practically molested you last night":** "Hot Tracks: Robin Thicke," *Vanity Fair*, November 2013.

10   **"[Cyrus] is a cheap act, no doubt about it":** "Miley Cyrus, Steubenville and Culture Run Amok," *Washington Post*, September 2, 2013.

10   **"I was ready to dismiss the 'let's condemn Miley' parade":** "The Verdict on Hannah and the Montana Judge," *USA Today*, August 29, 2013.

15   NICKI MINAJ'S BUTT EXPOSED IN SHEER JUMPSUIT: "Nicki Minaj's Butt Exposed in Sheer Jumpsuit During Dublin Concert," Katrina Mitzielotis, *Hollywood Life*, April 1, 2015.

15   EVEN NICKI MINAJ ISN'T SURE: "Even Nicki Minaj Isn't

Sure if Her Butt Is Photoshopped or Not," Jaleesa Jones, *USA Today*, August 10, 2015.

15   **NICKI MINAJ BUTT IMPLANT RUMORS:** "Nicki Minaj Butt Implant Rumors Are True!," *Rumorfix*, May 26, 2015.

15   **NICKI MINAJ FIRES BACK AT HATERS:** "Nicki Minaj Fires Back at Haters Who Say Her Butt Is the Reason She's Famous," Sarah Lindig, *Elle*, December 14, 2015.

15   **"a stripper who also knows how to rap":** "There Is Nothing Funny or Smart About That Viral Nicki Minaj 'Parody' Video," Caitlin Dewey, *Washington Post*, September 17, 2015.

16   **It was only in 2015, after a good eight or nine years:** This raises a few questions about gender identity, which I think are important to address. Featuring a non-binary celebrity in a book about how the media treats *women* risks misgendering that celebrity, if only by implication. However, Miley was perceived as female—and therefore treated as female by the media—for most of her time in the public eye. Media misogyny also still impacts her, because some people perceive her body and her gender presentation as feminine. I'll leave it to genderqueer readers to decide how well I've dealt with this complexity, but I do want to be clear that it is my aim to deal with it without consigning Miley to the wrong gender. One of the most maddening things about sexism, after all, is that it somehow manages to punish everyone who is not a cisgender man.

16   **"I don't relate to being boy or girl":** "Free to Be Miley," *Paper Magazine*, June 2015.

17   **"half the town" and "usurping bitch":** "The Vision of Liberty," as quoted in *The Cambridge Companion to Mary Wollstonecraft*, pp. 180–81.

17   **"much amiss in the head":** "Wollstonecraft and Fuseli," Robert Browning.

17   **"unsexed," "maniac," "no sense of guilt," and "whom no decorum checked":** "The Unsex'd Females," Richard Polwhele.

17   **"scripture, archly framed":** "The Vision of Liberty."

18   **"*Rights of Woman*, which the superficial fancied to be profound":** "The Anti-Jacobin Review, and Protestant Advocate: Or, Monthly Political and Literary Censor," p. 95.

21   **"I wish one moment that I had never heard of the cruelties":** "The Love Letters of Mary Wollstonecraft to Gilbert Imlay."

23   **"William hath penn'd a waggon-load of stuff":** "The Vision of Liberty," as quoted in *The Cambridge Companion to Mary Wollstonecraft*, pp. 180–81.

24   **"Come, from those livid limbs withdraw your gaze":** "The Unsex'd Females, A Poem," Rev. Richard Polwhele.

24   **"Much amiss in the head, Dear":** "Wollstonecraft and Fuseli," Robert Browning.

25   **"The biographer does not mention many of her amours":** "The Anti-Jacobin Review," p. 97.

26   **"Her works will be read with disgust":** Quoted in *A Bookshelf of Our Own: Books that Changed Women's Lives*, Deborah G. Felder, p. 23.

27   **"[Their] advocacy of Woman's cause becomes mere**

detriment": "Mary Wollstonecraft and the Critics, 1788–2001, Vol. 2," Harriet Devine Jump, p. 98.

28   **"This post exists to warn you to be cautious of Zoe"**: "The Zoe Post," thezoepost.wordpress.com/.

28   **"I *very* much align with SJ [social justice]"**: "This Guy's Embarrassing Relationship Drama Is Killing the 'Gamer' Identity," *Vice*, August 29, 2014.

29   **He would casually admit on Twitter that he calculated the odds**: "Eron Gjoni, Hateful Boyfriend," *Idle Dilettante*, December 6, 2014.

30   **"cheated on her boyfriend for calculated professional advancement"**: "Feminist Bullies Are Tearing the Gaming Industry Apart," *Breitbart*, September 1, 2014.

30   **"Next time she shows up at a conference"**: "Zoe Quinn's Depression Quest," *New Yorker*, September 9, 2015.

32   **"the Internet masses [have] found a new vice"**: "We'll Always Have Paris: The Rise and Fall of the Celebrity Sex Tape," *Slate*, June 24, 2015.

33   **"whore"**: "Why Must Miley Cyrus and Rihanna Act like Whores?," *Daily Mail*, October 4, 2013.

33   **"idea of a woman: a cleavage-boosting corset"**: "What Makes a Woman," *New York Times*, June 6, 2015.

33   **"sexual titillation for men"**: "Why Beyoncé shouldn't inspire feminists, despite her VMAs performance," *The Independent*, August 25, 2015.

33   **"wearing these stripper outfits onstage"**: "Stop Policing and Questioning Beyoncé's Feminist Credentials," *Mic*, May 17, 2015.

CHAPTER 2: NEED

38   **"The Teen Anti–'Train Wreck'"**: "Taylor Swift: The Teen Anti–'Train Wreck,'" *PopEater*, September 11, 2009.

39   **"Where's the romance?"**: "Taylor Swift in Wonderland," *Rolling Stone*, October 25, 2012.

39   **"'I wouldn't wear tiny amounts of clothing in my real life'"**: "Taylor Swift interview: 'I Won't Do Sexy Shoots,'" *Telegraph*, April 3, 2011.

39   **"You wouldn't find any naked pictures"**: *Rolling Stone*, October 15, 2012.

39   **"[Swift] isn't a person who's going to wake up"**: "Taylor Swift Gets Some Mud on Her Boots," *New York Times*, March 15, 2013.

39   **"Honestly, if somebody wants to criticize me"**: "Five Questions with Taylor Swift," *Seventeen*, January 20, 2009.

40   **"some clingy, insane, desperate girlfriend"**: "Taylor Swift's Telltale Heart," *Vanity Fair*, March 1, 2013.

40   **"Taylor Swift—HAS SHE LOST HER MIND?!?"**: "Taylor Swift—HAS SHE LOST HER MIND?!?," *TMZ*, 2012.

40   **"Taylor Swift Is a Psycho"**: "Taylor Swift Is a Psycho," *Thought Catalog*, October 25, 2012.

40   **"Seven Crazy Taylor Swift Girlfriend Moves"**: "7 Crazy Taylor Swift Girlfriend Moves in 2012," *The Frisky*, December 20, 2014.

40   **"Bad Seed of music"**: "Taylor Swift Is an Evil and Cruel Torturer," *DListed*, October 22, 2012.

41   **"Why can't I keep a guy?"**: "Q: Is Taylor Swift Turning Into Jennifer Aniston," *Stereogum*, January 23, 2014.

41   **"America's Favorite Spinster"**: "The Life of the Pity Party," *New York Magazine*, September 19, 2012.

42   **"the ex-*Friends* star has a habit"**: "Jennifer Aniston is 'clingy,'" *CelebrityFix*, January 7, 2008.

42   **"Jennifer Aniston's latest romance"**: "Jennifer Aniston's New Man Justin Theroux Seeing His Ex Behind Her Back—Are They Doomed?," *Hollywood Life*, July 13, 2011.

42   **"Jennifer Aniston is apparently suffering from PTSD"**: "Jennifer Aniston Forced to Watch Angelina Jolie and Brad Pitt Having Sex in 'Mr. and Mrs. Smith'—Freaks Out," *Celeb Dirty Laundry*, January 27, 2014.

43   **Eighty-seven percent of stalkers are male:** April 1998 National Violence Against Women Survey, www.svfree nyc.org/faq_question_40.html.

43   **In 2008, 45 percent of all female murder victims were killed by a partner:** Department of Justice, Bureau of Justice Statistics. www.cnn.com/2013/12/06/us/domestic-intimate-partner-violence-fast-facts/.

44   **"I Slept With a Crazy Woman"**: "Rebound: I Slept With a Crazy Woman," *xoJane*, April 17, 2012.

47   **"Literature cannot be the business of a woman's life"**: "Charlotte Brontë and Robert Southey: A Correspondence," Rich Byrne.

49   **"He is professor of rhetoric"**: *Selected Letters*, Charlotte Brontë, ed. Margaret Smith.

50   **"intellectual superiority, an imperious temper":** *The Se-cret of Charlotte Brontë,* Fredericka McDonald.

50   **"My youth is leaving me":** *The Life of Charlotte Brontë,* Elizabeth Gaskell.

52   **Some people even believe she may have spoken to him about her earlier attempts:** *The Brontë Myth,* Lucasta Miller.

55   **"Je me vengerai":** "'I Pine Away' . . . Charlotte Bronte's Romantic Obsession," *Guardian,* October 24, 2015.

56   **"truly offensive and sensual spirit":** "Mr. Bell's New Novel," *The Rambler: A Catholic Journal and Review of Home and Foreign Literature*

56   **Obviously, this is Thackeray:** Thackeray's daughter brought it up in her memoirs, specifically in her description of meeting Charlotte: "This then is the authoress, the unknown power whose books have set all London talking, reading, speculating; some people even say our father wrote the books—the wonderful books," Anne Isabella Thackeray Ritchie, *Chapters from Some Memoirs.*

59   **"dating police":** "Julian Assange Captured by World's Dating Police," *Huffington Post,* December 7, 2010.

59   **"Are you a scorned woman?":** "Anita Hill: 'We can evolve.' But the same questions are being asked," *Washington Post,* April 3, 2014.

59   **Meanwhile, lawyer John Doggett testified that Hill was delusional:** "The Thomas Nomination: Excerpts from Affidavit About Hill," *New York Times,* October 12, 1991.

60   **When questioned, she covered for him:** "Bloodied and

bruised Amy Winehouse stands by husband who 'saved her life,'" *Daily Mail*, August 24, 2007.

60   **"you'd be dead because you weren't together":** "Up All Night with Amy Winehouse," *Rolling Stone*, August 10, 2008.

61   **A "Rihanna Deserved It" T-shirt was sold on Cafe-Press:** "T-Shits," *Jezebel*, February 12, 2009.

61   **And in one survey of two hundred teenagers, 46 percent blamed Rihanna:** "Teenage Girls Stand by Their Man," *New York Times*, March 18, 2009.

61   **"Im a women myself and I never want to get beat by a man":** "Don't you think Rihanna probably deserved it? . . ." *Yahoo: Answers*.

61   **"I decided it was more important for me to be happy":** "Rihanna Says She Is Back with Chris Brown," *New York Times*, January 20, 2013.

61   **"Gone [are] the days":** "Rihanna—a Bad Role Model?" *Tell Tales*, March 12, 2012.

62   **"telling young people everywhere that domestic abuse is healthy":** "Rihanna Shouldn't Take Chris Brown Back— He's a Violent Felon," *Hollywood Life*, August 20, 2012.

64   **"By every vessel he wrote":** *Villette*, Charlotte Brontë.

CHAPTER 3: MADNESS

68   **"When Kurt died, I just fell into this endless spiral":** "Inside the Mind of Courtney Love," *The Fix*, February 1, 2012.

69   **"there were people outside her house every day":**
      "Courtney Love Comes Out of Hiding," Dana Kennedy,
      Entertainment Weekly, August 12, 1994.

71   **"the city of incurable women":** *Invention of Hysteria: Charcot
      and the Photographic Iconography of La Salpêtrière*, Georges-Didi
      Huberman, p. 13.

73   **"the camera likes her":** "The Girls of Salpêtrière," Oliver
      Walusinski, MD, www.baillement.com/lettres/Girls_
      Salpêtrière.pdf.

73   **"She closes her eyes, her physiognomy denoting pos-
      session":** *Invention of Hysteria: Charcot and the Photographic Ico-
      nography of Salpêtrière*, Didi Huberman-Georges, p. 144.

75   **"tried to persuade me I was in love with my brother-
      in-law":** "Freud, Charcot and Hysteria: Lost in the Laby-
      rinth," Richard Webster, www.richardwebster.net/freud
      andcharcot.html.

81   **"those females least embedded in the male 'Culture'":**
      SCUM Manifesto, Valerie Solanas.

84   **it was Girodias who told the world that SCUM was an
      acronym:** The *Manifesto* has never been printed without ref-
      erence to Warhol; a mention of the shooting in the author
      bio or preface, a quote from Solanas about why she wasn't
      sorry on the back, or (in the e-book version I own) an actual
      photo of Warhol's scars on the cover.

85   **As art critic Catherine Lord points out:** "Wonder Waif
      Meets Super Neuter," Catherine Lord, www.ubuweb.com
      /historical/solanas/lord_on_solanas.pdf.

88   **In one study, recovering alcoholics with greater ten-dencies toward shame:** "Being Ashamed of Drinking Causes Relapse, Not Recovery," Maia Salavitz, *Time*, February 7, 2013.

CHAPTER 4: DEATH

92   **"No, no, no. I would never":** "Primetime: Special Edition," November 2002, www.youtube.com/watch?v=Omof KdmQSeo.

93   **"This interview . . . [from] when Whitney was still all drugged up":** "The 10 Best Moments from Whitney Houston's Infamous Diane Sawyer Interview," Matt Stopera, *BuzzFeed*, September 10, 2009.

94   **"The Most Disturbing Moment":** "The Most Disturbing Moment from Whitney Houston's 2002 Diane Sawyer Interview," James Crugnale, *Mediaite*, February 13, 2012.

95   ***NME Magazine,* which had nominated her:** "Amy Winehouse Up for Villain of the Year," *Now Magazine*, January 29, 2008.

95   **"little scabs that raid her face":** "Up All Night with Amy Winehouse," Claire Hoffman, *Rolling Stone*, July 10, 2008.

96   **"remarkable musical achievements were often overshadowed":** "Amy Winehouse's Death: A Troubled Star Gone Too Soon," Jenny Eliscu, *Rolling Stone*, July 24, 2011.

96   **the Elton John rewrite of "Candle in the Wind":** Which, of course, had been about Marilyn Monroe's death in the

first place; the celebrity death script was so well worked-out, by that point, that you only needed to make a few lyrical adjustments.

96   **which became the best-selling single of all time:** "Elton John: Biography," *Rolling Stone.*

96   **In 1999, *The New York Times* endorsed author Sally Bedel Smith's posthumous diagnosis:** "Shrinking the Princess," Frank Kermode, *New York Times,* August 22, 1999.

97   **"kissing Hitler":** *Billy Wilder in Hollywood,* Maurice Zolotow, p. 263.

97   **"I'm the only director who ever made two pictures with Monroe":** Ibid., p. 264.

97   **"I have been besieged by newspapermen":** Ibid., pp. 265–66.

98   **A *Ladies' Home Journal* profile of her was killed for being too sympathetic:** "The Woman Who Will Not Die," Gloria Steinem, PBS, 1986.

98   **"An actor is supposed to be a sensitive instrument":** "Last Talk with a Lonely Girl," Richard Meryman, *Time,* August 17, 1962 (republished in the *Guardian*).

98   **"including the half-drunk bottle of champagne she used to wash the pills down":** "The Things She Left Behind," Sam Kashner, *Vanity Fair,* September 30, 2008.

99   **"the 'Cadillac of caskets'":** "Death of Marilyn Monroe," Wikipedia.

99   **"I'm a sucker for blondes and she is the ultimate blonde":** "Hugh Hefner Talks About His Memories of Marilyn Monroe," *CBS Los Angeles,* August 3, 2012.

99   **"If I croak, if you don't put me upside down over Marilyn":** "For Sale: Eternity with Marilyn Monroe," Jeff Gottlieb, *Los Angeles Times*, August 14, 2009.

99   **Bidding started at $500,000:** It's tempting to judge Elsie for this—the eBay auction is a particularly tacky touch—but you really shouldn't. Given the nature of his last requests, Poncher is lucky his wife didn't sell his skeleton to the nearest haunted house.

101   **"I wish I was dead already":** "Lana Del Rey: 'I Wish I Was Dead Already,'" Tim Jonze, *Guardian*, June 12, 2014.

102   **"I'm a big jazz aficionado":** "Love, Death and Jazz: Seven Outtakes from Our Lana Del Rey Interview," *Fader*, June 20, 2014.

102   **"I was playing a gig in New Jersey, walking across the yard":** *Billie Holiday: Wishing on the Moon*, Donald Clarke, chapter 18.

103   **"And I said to myself, new angle, new angle, new angle":** Ibid.

104   **"I could play in theaters and sing to an audience of kids":** *Lady Sings the Blues*, Billie Holiday and William Dufty, chapter 19.

104   **Articles "by" Billie Holiday, on the topic of her addiction:** *Billie Holiday: The Musician and the Myth*, John Szwed, chapter 2.

106   **"I'll never forget that night":** Holiday and Dufty, chapter 1.

107   **"[Instead] of treating me and Mom like somebody who went to the cops for help":** Ibid.

107 **"beat the shit out of her so she sings good":** Clarke, chapter 14.

108 **"Everybody was happy about the crowds":** Holiday and Dufty, chapter 20.

109 **"When I sing, it affects me so much I get sick":** Holiday and Dufty, chapter 9.

110 **"There is so much of human suffering, sensitivity and music in her voice":** Szwed, chapter 1.

110 **"This reviewer is no squeamish prude":** Ibid.

111 **"My book is just a bitch":** Ibid.

111 **"I'm not supposed to get a toothache":** Holiday and Dufty, chapter 23.

112 **"We're all doomed, baby":** Szwed, chapter 1.

115 **In the four weeks directly after her death:** "Effect of the Death of Diana, Princess of Wales, on suicide and deliberate self-harm," bjp.rcpsych.org/content/bjprcpsych /177/5/463.full.pdf.

115 **The overall U.S. suicide rate rose by 12 percent:** "The Science Behind Suicide Contagion," Margot Sanger-Katz, *New York Times*, August 13, 2014.

CHAPTER 5: SHUT UP

122 **"probably the stupidest thing I ever did":** "Tara Reid Opens Up About Plastic Surgery," Amy Bonawitz, *CBS News*, October 13, 2006.

122 **"I was smiling like a fool and people were snapping away":** Ibid.

123 **"'moving on' from the botched breast augmentation"**: "Tara Reid: The Truth About My Body," Amy Eliza Keith, *People*, November 10, 2008.

123 **"It wasn't really the pictures that hurt me"**: Ibid.

124 **"I figured, I'm in Hollywood"**: "Tara Reid Gets 'Ugliest' Breast Surgery Repaired," *ABC News*, abcnews.go.com /Health/story?id=2573773&page=1.

124 **"I couldn't wear a bikini"**: "Tara Reid Opens Up About Plastic Surgery," *CBS News*.

126 **"the first American singer-songwriter"**: "Lost Women Found," Robert Forster, *The Weekly*, June 2009.

127 **"you are bringing up the greatest critic we heard of in America"**: "Vanishing Act," Paul Collins, *Lapham's Quarterly*.

128 **she had been so sure that her popularity would "burn out"**: "Back from the Wilderness," Grace Macaskill, *Scottish Daily Mail*, November 19, 2005.

129 **"Anon, who wrote so many poems without signing them, was often a woman"**: *A Room of One's Own*, Virginia Woolf, chapter 3.

130 **"It was the relic of the sense of chastity"**: Ibid.

130 **"I was told you had once some thoughts of bringing Fanny out as a professional singer"**: *The Letters of Charlotte Brontë, Vol. 2*, ed. Margaret Smith, p. 312.

131 **"go back up into your quarters, and take up your own work"**: "The Public Voice of Women," Mary Beard, *London Review of Books*, March 20, 2014.

131   **"Let the woman learn in silence, with all subjection":** 1 Timothy 2.11 and 2.12, King James version.

131   **"angry woman who, by brawling and wrangling amongst her neighbours":** Duhaime's Law Dictionary, www.duhaime.org/LegalDictionary/C/Common-Scold.aspx.

133   **"[Women] are not even now as concerned":** *A Room of One's Own*, Virginia Woolf, chapter 3.

134   **"As this is the first time that I ever took my pen":** "Letter from a Fugitive Slave," *New York Daily Tribune*, June 21, 1853.

135   **"I have not the Courage":** *Harriet Jacobs: A Life*, Jean Fagan Yellin, p. 129.

135   **"Would you not think that Southern Women had cause to despise":** "Letter from a Fugitive Slave."

135   **"the spelling I believe was every word":** Yellin, p. 13.

136   **Historian John Blassingame:** Blassingame often comes off as a villain in this story, due to his dismissiveness. In fact, he's one of the more respected and accomplished historians in this field—and, when Yellin found evidence that proved him wrong, he supported her fully.

136   **"The story is too melodramatic":** "To Be Raped, Bred or Abused," Henry Louis Gates Jr., *New York Times*, November 22, 1987.

137   **"Reader, my story ends with freedom":** *Incidents in the Life of a Slave Girl*, Harriet Jacobs, chapter 41.

138   **"Though impelled by a natural craving for human sympathy":** *Incidents in the Life of a Slave Girl*, Harriet Jacobs, Appendix.

139 **"Dear Amy if it was the life of a Heroine":** Harriet Jacobs to Amy Post, Yale archive.

141 **"Pity me, and pardon me, O virtuous reader!":** *Incidents in the Life of a Slave Girl*, Harriet Jacobs, chapter 10.

142 **"I don't think I changed fifty words":** *Harriet Jacobs: A Life*, Jean Fagan Yellin, p. 141.

143 **"The brave deeds of Margaret Garner":** Ibid., p. 261.

145 **One 2001 study found that women:** "Men Rule: The Continued Under-Representation of Women in Politics," Jennifer L. Lawless and Richard L. Fox, *Women in Politics Institute & School of Public Affairs*.

146 **when men and women are deliberately given equal speaking time:** "Language Myth #6: Women Talk More than Men," Janet Holmes, PBS.

CHAPTER 6: SPEAK UP

149 **"Dignity / Down Boy":** "Hilary Duff Stuffs Backpacks; Plus Lindsay Lohan, Fabolous, Foxy Brown, Paris Hilton, Britney Spears & More, In For the Record," *MTV News*, June 14, 2007.

150 **"[referred] to blocking out negativity":** "Britney Spears Names New Album 'Blackout,'" *Reuters*, October 6, 2007.

150 **"I don't really want to talk about it any more":** *The Late Show with David Letterman*, September 21, 2007.

151 **"Now see everyone's watching":** "The Secret History of Britney Spears' Lost Album," Hunter Schwarz, *Buzzfeed*, April 27, 2014.

151   **"an unwritten rule"**: "Bloodshy & Avant," Cafe.se, June
       16, 2008.

152   **When Mary Wollstonecraft was being demolished:**
       Which, of course, raises the question of what an unflatter-
       ing photo of Mary Wollstonecraft would look like. I choose
       to believe they'd have gone with the classic upskirt; those
       eighteenth-century dresses are pretty bulky, but if you
       crouched down low enough, I'm sure you could catch Mary
       showing ankle.

154   ***"Why did you marry the man you did? (or date the man you
       do?)"***: "How to Start Your Own Consciousness-Raising
       Group," Chicago Women's Liberation Union, 1971.

155   **"For every scientific study we quote"**: "Consciousness-
       Raising; a Radical Weapon," Kathie Sarachild.

157   **"Our meetings were called coffee klatches"**: Ibid.

158   **"It is at this point a political action to tell it like it is"**:
       "The Personal Is Political," Carol Hanisch.

158   **"In the absence of feminist activity"**: "The Tyranny of
       Tyranny," Cathy Levine.

159   **"a pretty young mother of two children was found in a
       London flat"**: "Books: The Blood Jet Is Poetry," *Time*, June
       10, 1966.

159   **"A man in black with a Meinkampf look"**: *The Collected
       Poems of Sylvia Plath*, ed. Ted Hughes, pp. 222–24.

161   **"a mint / by becoming Plath's posthumous editor"**:
       Rough Magic: A Biography of Sylvia Plath, Paul Alexander, chap-
       ter 6.

165 **"Sexually predatory, rabidly ambitious, mentally unstable":** "The poet caught in the eye of the tornado," *Sunday Times*, October 14, 2001.

165 **"Hysterical insanity, whatever its momentary erotic appeal":** *Sylvia Plath*, ed. Harold Bloom, p. 2.

166 **"[there] is a special place in hell for narcissistic mothers":** "Narcissistic Mothers," Cyndi Lopez, *PsychCentral*.

166 **"Plath's poetry can be seen to be preoccupied with 'borderline' themes":** "Sylvia Plath and the Depression Continuum," Anthony Ryle, September 2003.

167 *Infinite Jest*, **like** *The Bell Jar*: The books' origin stories are so similar that, upon close consideration, the distinguishing line between male genius and female madness would seem to be "has footnotes."*   * Lots and *lots* of footnotes.

171 **"It Happened to Me":** "It Happened to Me: I Let an Old Rich White Man Bankroll My Life . . . Even Though He Was Racist," Anonymous, *xoJane*, May 2, 2014.

171 **"I'm Being Stalked and Terrorized":** "It Happened to Me: I'm Being Stalked and Terrorized Because of My Fat Acceptance Movie," Lindsey Averill, *xoJane*, April 25, 2014.

172 **"I Was Suspended from My Teaching Job":** "It Happened to Me: I Was Suspended from My Teaching Job for Being Transgender," Laura Jane Klug, *xoJane*, April 16, 2014.

172 **"It Happened to Me: A Gynecologist":** "It Happened to Me: A Gynecologist Found a Ball of Cat Hair in My Vagina," Michelle Barrow, *xoJane*, September 2, 2015.

172   **"a place where women go to be selfish"**: "Mixed Reviews for Jane Pratt's New Website," Alex Eichler, *The Atlantic Wire*, May 16, 2011.

CHAPTER 7: SCAPEGOAT

182   **"now and for the foreseeable future"**: "A.P. Says It Wants
to Know Everything About Britney Spears," Brian Stelter,
New York Times, January 14, 2008.

182   **"one shot of Britney slowly spiraling into insanity"**:
"Bald Britney Spears Was the Dot-Com Boom Era for Paparazzi," American Ex-Pap, *Defamer*.

183   **"habitual, frequent and continuous drug user"**: "The
Tragedy of Britney Spears," Vanessa Grigoriadis, *Rolling
Stone*, February 21, 2008.

184   **"Britney Spears extends a honeyed thigh across the
length of the sofa"**: "Britney Spears, Teen Queen: *Rolling
Stone*'s 1999 Cover Story," Steven Daly, *Rolling Stone*.

185   **"You want to be a good example for kids out there"**:
Ibid.

185   **"Spears' pink T-shirt is distended"**: Ibid.

188   **"This guy jumps up on the stage"**: "Britney Spears: The
Girl Can't Help It," Chris Mundy, *Rolling Stone*, May 25,
2000.

188   **"I don't want to be part of someone's *Lolita* thing"**:
Ibid.

188   **"Alone in the house one night, she hid from a prowler"**:
Daly.

190   COCAINE, MORE SECRET SURGERY: "You HAVE to

See Kylie Jenner's Reaction to a Mag Cover Claiming She's 'Destroyed by Fame,'" Hannah Orenstein, *Seventeen*.

193 **"former employees remember [him] laying out a four-act cover drama":** "How *In Touch*'s Duggars Coverage Has Changed Tabloid Journalism," Anne Helen Petersen, *Buzzfeed*, June 16, 2015.

195 **"some little woman, standing by my man":** "Hillary's First Joint Interview—Next to Bill in '92," *CBS News*, February 1, 2013.

195 **"stayed home and baked cookies and had teas":** "Nightline Transcript: Making Hillary Clinton an Issue," PBS, March 26, 1992.

195 **"a buffoon, an insult to most women":** Ibid.

195 **"The damage had been done":** Ibid.

195 **"Then, there's Clinton":** Ibid.

196 **"lit up a cigarette to punish her smoke-allergic husband":** "Hillary Clinton: First Lady of the Lamp," *Snopes.com*.

198 **"she engaged in sexual relations but he did not":** "*Washington Post* Special Report: *The Starr Report*," *Washington Post*.

199 **"I was never going to see the president again" and "pain in the neck" and "many phone calls" and "distraught and sometimes in tears" and "highly emotional lady":** Ibid.

200 **"Any normal person would have walked away from this":** Ibid.

200 **"blow-job queen":** "How Does It Feel to Be America's Blow-Job Queen?," Ian Rothkerch, *Salon*, March 1, 2002.

201   **"I just knew he was in love with me"**: *Starr Report.*

201   **"My first job out of college was at the White House"**:
"Shame and Survival," Monica Lewinsky, *Vanity Fair*, May
31, 2014.

201   **"Isn't it interesting that Bill doesn't go for women"**:
"New York Supergals Love That Naughty Prez," Francine
Prose, *New York Observer*, February 9, 1998.

201   **"Hillary Clinton changed her hairstyle one million
times"**: Ibid.

201   **"I think [Hillary] would actually be more effective"**:
Ibid.

202   **"she has so much power over his mind"**: Ibid.

202   **"narcissistic Loony-Toon"**: "Hillary Clinton: Monica
Lewinsky a 'Narcissistic Loony Toon,'" *CBS News*, February 10, 2014.

202   **"Hillary Clinton wanted it on record"**: "Shame and Survival," *Vanity Fair.*

205   **"just another crackhead"**: "Didn't she almost have it all?,"
Rebecca Traister, *Salon*, April 12, 2006.

207   **She is not allowed to use her cell phone**: "Control of
Britney Spears' Life Is Her Father's Prerogative," *Los Angeles Times*, February 27, 2009.

207   **"a prisoner"**: "Why Do We Talk About Britney Spears
Like She's Not a Prisoner?," Michelle Dean, *Flavorwire*, December 11, 2013.

207   **"a feminist role model for single working mothers"**:
"Miss American Dream," Taffy Brodesser-Akner, *Medium.*

208   **"Oh, I loved it"**: Ibid.

209 **"most admired woman anywhere in the world"**: "Gallup: Hillary Clinton ranked most-admired woman in U.S. for record 20th year," Michael Walsh, *Yahoo!*, December 28, 2015.

209 **"somebody who can take her into a room"**: "Keith Olbermann's Idea for Beating Hillary: Literally Beating Hillary," Rachel Sklar, *Huffington Post*, May 2, 2008.

209 **"Stop Hillary!"**: "Stop Hillary!," Doug Henwood, *Harper's Magazine*.

209 **a Photoshopped image of her eating a baby**: Doug Henwood, Twitter.

CHAPTER 8: REVOLUTIONARY

215 **"Anne ux. Richard Walker being cast out of the church of Boston"**: *Curious Punishments of Bygone Days*, Alice Morse Earle, p. 74.

216 **"No brawling wives, no furious wenches"**: Ibid., p. 16.

216 **"One of the latest, and certainly the most notorious"**: Ibid., p. 37.

220 **8 percent in 1960**: "Record Share of Americans Have Never Married," Wendy Wang and Kim Parker, Pew Research Center.

220 **as compared to 28 percent in 1990**: "The New Demography of American Motherhood," Gretchen Livingston and D'Vera Cohn, Pew Research Center, May 6, 2010.

220 **"the joy of having children"**: Ibid.

221 **"When you agree to meet a strange man in a strange**

place": "Mitchell: Rape case sends mixed messages on prostitution," Mary Mitchell, *Chicago Sun-Times*, September 12, 2015.

222　**"All survivors of rape"**: "What you should do instead of victim-blaming sex workers who report being raped," Anne Theriault, *Daily Dot*, May 16, 2015.

222　**"Even if you're a whore, you don't want to be raped"**: *Lady Sings the Blues*, Holiday & Dufty, chapter 1.

223　**"change 'bitch' to 'whore'"**: *Billie Holiday: The Musician and the Myth*, Szwed, chapter 1.

226　**"I have seen a number of wise men"**: *Theroigne de Mericourt: A Melancholic Woman during the French Revolution*, Élisabeth Roudinesco, p. 28.

227　**"I had always been extremely humiliated"**: "Madness and Revolution: The Sad Life of Theroigne de Mericourt," *History and Other Thoughts*, May 2015.

228　**"This nymph is a trollop"**: Roudinesco, p. 31.

228　**"Theroigne in the district"**: Ibid., p. 56.

228　**"the rights of a man over his wife"**: Ibid., p. 39.

229　**"I cannot bring myself to admit"**: Ibid., p. 61.

229　**"I left the French Revolution without too much regret"**: Ibid., p. 43.

230　**"barbaric queen, adulterous wife"**: *Citizens: A Chronicle of the French Revolution*, Simon Schama, pp. 224–25.

230　**"all its members have drawn from the vagina of the Austrian Woman"**: "The Royal Dildo," Leah Marie Brown.

230　**"The Royal Dildo"**: Ibid.

232 **"the greatest of all the joys of the Pere Duchesne"**: Schama, p. 800.

233 **"I propose that each section appoint six women citizens"**: Roudinesco, p. 134.

234 **"I have neither paper nor light"**: Ibid., p. 147.

234 **"She outlined a few words"**: Ibid., p. 172

235 **"She acted as if she were involved in very important matters"**: Ibid.

235 **"gave herself to various leaders of the party"**: Ibid., pp. 170–71.

237 **"In all that she did"**: *The Song Machine*, John Seabrook, chapter 7.

237 **"She's fifteen years old"**: Ibid.

244 **"It is perfectly simple"**: Roudinesco, pp. 96–97.

245 **"If we wish to preserve our liberty"**: Ibid.

Index

About the Author

SADY DOYLE founded the blog *Tiger Beatdown* in 2008. Her work has appeared in *In These Times*, *The Guardian*, *Elle*, *The Atlantic*, *Slate*, *Buzzfeed*, *Rookie*, and lots of other places around the Internet. She won the first-ever Women's Media Center Social Media Award by popular vote in 2011. She lives in Brooklyn, New York. *Trainwreck* is her first book.